LAST DANCE OF THE VESTRIS

L + H

CLINT OLIVIER

Copyright © 2013 by Clint Olivier

All rights reserved.

ISBN-10: 1475223129

ISBN-13: 978-1475223125

For my son, Conrad James Olivier

CONTENTS

	Foreword	vii
	Preface	ix
1	"Be Careful What You Put in the Log"	1
2	"There is Something the Matter"	17
3	"Have You Anything to Communicate?"	21
4	"The Ship is Sinking, but Very Slowly"	31
5	"Don't Take Time to Shave"	34
6	"Get Up, Charlie, This is Serious"	42
7	"Stay With Me, I'm Going to Live"	46
8	"Do the Best You Can"	52
9	"Do They Really Mean it?"	65
10	"My God, My God, I am Not to Blame for This"	73

CONTENTS

11	"Look, She's Gone"	85
12	"We Don't Want No Women in Here"	91
13	"I've Got to Give Up"	96
14	"Take Hold of One End, and I'll Take the Other"	101
15	"Thank God You Are Safe"	120
16	"They Were Murderers"	134
17	"He Proved Himself a Hero"	150
18	"Only The Strong Had a Chance of Being Saved"	160
19	"These Men All Died in Storm and Terror"	167
	Appendix A: "The Gold Ship"	170
	Appendix B: Passengers and Crew	176
	Appendix C: Deck Plans	183
	Bibliography	186
	Acknowledgements	190
	About the Author	192

FOREWORD

The steamship *Vestris* sank during heavy weather in 1928. There was an appalling loss of life, the majority of which were women and all thirteen children who were on board.

Last Dance of the Vestris is the well researched, riveting story of a tragedy that may well have been prevented by adherence to British regulations already in place, but disregarded by the Lamport and Holt Line's ships based in the United States. Intrigue enters the story when the question is raised of whether the *Vestris* was overloaded. Founder William J. Lamport was instrumental in the framing of the first Merchant Shipping Act in the United Kingdom which resulted in the successful campaign by Samuel Plimsoll, Member of Parliament, to improve conditions of seamen and safety at sea by the adoption of the Load Line in 1876.

However, devastating accidents are rarely caused by a single action. Clint Olivier's portrayal of the inquiry will possibly make you pause and consider that even today, poor loading and a disregard for proper checks on safety equipment could mean the difference between a successful voyage or one filled with severe consequences of shock and grief.

Those lost at sea have no known graves. This book serves as a memorial to the tragic demise of the passengers and crew of the *Vestris*. As a former seafarer, I commend and thank Clint Olivier for remembering them.

> Commodore R. W. Warwick OBE FNI MNM
> Somerset – 2013

PREFACE

Some years ago, I visited the Hotel Queen Mary in Long Beach, California with my wife and son. While looking at the lifeboat exhibit, I noticed a haunting photograph among the artifacts in the case. The black-and-white shot showed a group of men trying to launch a lifeboat from the deck of a perilously listing ship. The caption beneath the photograph identified it simply as the sinking of the *S.S. Vestris*, but it wasn't enough. I wanted to know more.

At home later that day, the websites of the usual online booksellers came up empty for the *Vestris*. In addition to the dozens of volumes written about the *Titanic* and *Lusitania*, I discovered even the lesser-known wrecks of the *Morro Castle* and *Empress of Ireland* have been the subjects of several books. No author ever attempted to tell the story of the *Vestris*. So began an odyssey that culminated in this volume. As I began my research, I was shocked—the account was eerily familiar to another shipwreck I once read about. Readers with only a basic knowledge of shipping history will recognize the story:

> She was built in Belfast, Ireland and left on her maiden voyage in 1912, one of three sister ships created to bring her owners prestige and profit. No expense was spared in making

her thoroughly modern and beautiful. The ship was grand, but she was also believed to be extraordinarily safe. At one point, some of her safety features were the subject of an article in Britain's *Shipbuilder* magazine.

On her fatal voyage, she was commanded by the shipping line's senior captain. There were wealthy and famous passengers on board. Steaming in the North Atlantic on a Sunday night, they were warm, dry and safe until the fatal encounter. On the bridge, nothing could be done to avoid contact. Some passengers felt a slight vibration, while still others slept through the crash. Far below, engineers worked frantically to stop the inflow of seawater. The use of pumps only served to prolong the agony.

When it came time to abandon ship, no alarm bells rang. Word to take to the boats spread from person to person. Instead of offering helpful and potentially lifesaving information, cheerful officers told frightened passengers not to worry. However, the captain *was* worried. He knew his ship was doomed, so he ordered his young wireless officers to send the distress signal. Miles away, a brave skipper received the cry for help and made full speed to the scene of the wreck. Another, much closer vessel was unable to hear the SOS.

The captain ordered "Women and children first." With the deck at an ever-worsening angle, sailors managed to swing out and load the lifeboats. Husbands and wives were forever separated when men were refused entry. Even so, most boats left the ship woefully below capacity. The captain went down with his vessel. So did the hero wireless officer. Survivors were picked up and taken to New York where they were mobbed by reporters. The name of the hero Marconi man was inscribed on the Wireless Officers Monument in Battery Park.

PREFACE

Remarkably, the account can describe the loss of either the *R.M.S. Titanic* or the *S.S. Vestris*. Their stories bring to mind Mark Twain's observation, "History does not repeat itself, but it often rhymes." The *Titanic* and the *Vestris* rhyme very closely.

Apart from the disparity in death tolls—roughly 1,300 more died on the *Titanic*—the most glaring difference between the two ships can be found in their respective legacies. The *Titanic* has achieved mythical status while the *Vestris* and her passengers and crew are mostly lost to history. That is a tragedy in itself. In an effort to bring them back from the brink of the abyss, I have recreated the sinking of the *Vestris*, the sometimes ridiculous efforts employed to save her, the cowardice and heroism displayed by members of her crew and the dramatic stories of her passengers as they struggled to survive.

It may be interesting to note the pleasing system adopted by the line in the naming of its ships. They are named after persons who have become distinguished in some branch of music, literature or art. For example, the magnificent *S.S. Vestris* was named after a family whose exquisite dancing many years ago won enthusiastic plaudits from all the stages of Europe.

—From a Lamport and Holt brochure

CHAPTER ONE

"Be Careful What You Put In the Log"

New York Harbor came to life with the arrival of the November sun. Its rays lent color to the liner's baby blue and white funnel, glistened through her dewy rigging and illuminated the British Red Ensign flapping gently above her aft rail. For anyone who happened to be cruising the North River past the bustling piers at Hoboken, New Jersey, there was no mistaking the ship's name. Emblazoned on her stern were two words: *Vestris, Liverpool.*

A courier from the Manhattan office of the Lamport and Holt Line made his way along Pier 14 and up the gangway with a package of official correspondence for the ship's master. His orders were inside: "The *Vestris* is due to sail at 3:45 p.m. to-morrow, Saturday, November 10th. Please have your vessel in readiness to proceed to sea at that time." As 59-year-old Captain William John Carey flipped through the packet, he learned his assignment was the same as it ever was—to safely navigate his ship, its cargo and passengers to the usual South American ports and back. It was a route he knew well. Outbound, the

Vestris would first call at Rio de Janeiro, then Montevideo and Buenos Aires. Homeward, the schedule would take the ship from the Argentine capital to Trinidad and on to Barbados before finally returning to New York. The round trip would take two months.

The cheerful Carey should have felt well-rested and ready to go to sea. This would be his first voyage back after spending two months leave at home in the Liverpool suburb of Great Crosby. For the Careys, serving the company was a family affair. One of their sons was captain of the *Raphael*; another was second officer of the *Leighton*. In addition, for four decades of reliable and honorable service to Lamport and Holt, the Waterford, Ireland native had been named Commodore of the Line.

Captain Carey was a model officer with a reputation for being a strict disciplinarian, but he was, nevertheless, admired and respected by his crews. His safety record was unblemished, except for an unavoidable mishap when the troopship he commanded was torpedoed during the Great War. Carey's heroism while the *Titian* was going down made him a living legend.[1] The captain made sure every last man was in a lifeboat before going back for the ship's cat. Passengers loved him because he always had a yarn or joke for whoever would listen. This fact wasn't lost on reporters who were known to approach Carey for news tidbits while the *Vestris* was in port. His image was even captured by an early newsreel camera as he stood on deck chatting with a passenger.

Carey and his ship had a lot in common. By 1928, the two were nearing the end of their respective careers, but both master and vessel remained effective at their jobs. Sixteen years after entering service, the *Vestris* was not only still popular with passengers; she was officially in good shape. The week before, a handful of inspectors from the U.S. Steamboat Inspection Service spent four days poking around the ship and eating heartily in her dining rooms before issuing a certificate of

---

[1] Carey and the *Titian* were victims of the Austro-Hungarian Empire's *U-14* under the command of Georg Johannes von Trapp, who would be best remembered for being patriarch of the Trapp Family Singers.

"BE CAREFUL WHAT YOU PUT IN THE LOG"

seaworthiness. However, apart from their acceptance of free food and quite possibly a few beers and glasses of Scotch here and there, the visit wasn't entirely on the up-and-up. In his report, Chief Inspector Edward Keane wrote the word "yes" in the blank that required the *Vestris's* fourteen lifeboats be lowered to the water and their releasing gear tested. Neither ever occurred.

Captain William J. Carey. (*Wide World*)

The inspectors believed they had a reasonable excuse for neglecting their duties—inconvenience. With coal barges pressed against one side of the ship and the dock against the other, there was no way the required test could be performed. Keane simply lied on the paperwork and moved on to the next item. The inspectors certified the lifeboats to be in perfect condition and outfitted with all the necessary equipment. They also found their releasing gear to be "without defect." Lastly, the men reported no broken portholes in the passenger cabins. When Keane and company went ashore, they became the second group of reputable inspectors to praise the *Vestris*. A little more than two months earlier, a representative of Lloyd's of London pronounced the ship to be in "very good" condition, awarding her a rating of "A-1."

LAST DANCE OF THE VESTRIS

For the moment, there remained quite literally a mountain of work to be done before Carey could take his vessel to sea. In an era of oil-fired ships, the coal-burning *Vestris* was a throwback. Hundreds of tons of coal still had to be brought on board in a filthy and labor-intensive process that involved pouring it through the ship's hull into bunkers. In addition, a great quantity of cargo was still waiting to be loaded.

As chief officer, Frank Johnson would oversee much of the work. Getting a cargo ship ready to go to sea was an assignment he was used to, but dealing with the challenges posed by a vessel full of passengers was not. Johnson's entire sixteen year career up to the time he joined the *Vestris* six months prior was spent on cargo ships. And there was an additional wrinkle in his life. The 34-year-old woke up Friday morning as first officer, but was promoted to chief that afternoon. There was no time for celebration. In addition to a host of new duties, Johnson found himself supervising three other young officers: First Officer John Bolger, Second Officer Leslie Watson and Third Officer Herbert Welland.

The newly-minted chief watched nearly three thousand tons of cargo come aboard, including sixty-eight cases of typewriters, eighty-six cases of cash registers, fifty-eight cases of tractor parts, toys, fresh fruit, steel office furniture, motorcycles, railroad materials, hosiery, General Motors auto parts and three new Chevrolets in massive crates. None of it was light. As each case was lifted into the holds, the *Vestris* dipped lower and lower in the murky water. Hundreds of trunks and suitcases were also added, but with the baggage room full, much of it was dumped haphazardly into unused passenger cabins. More than a thousand sacks of mail weighing fifty tons, along with ten pouches of diplomatic mail destined for embassies in Rio, Montevideo and Buenos Aires rounded out the load.

British vessels were limited in the amount of cargo that could be safely carried. Parliament was pressured to act when the badly-overloaded *S.S. London* sank in a storm in 1866 with the loss of more than two hundred lives. Eventually, the Merchant Shipping Act was passed and load lines were added to hulls to indicate whether a vessel was overloaded. Sometimes referred to as "Plimsoll lines," after the Member of Parliament who fought for their adoption, the marks were credited with saving hundreds of thousands of lives throughout the decades. Any owner who allowed his ship to sail "below her marks" could be sanctioned by the Board of Trade.

S.S. Vestris. Ticket prices from New York to Buenos Aires ranged from about $125 per person for a Third Class passage, to $235 for a Second Class berth to $785 for a First Class *Cabin de Luxe*. (*Associated Press*)

Although the *Vestris* hadn't been home to Liverpool for years, the ship was still bound by British law. Unfortunately, the lax atmosphere across the Pond turned out to be perfect for Lamport and Holt managers who largely encouraged overloading by ignoring it. The United States Government didn't regulate cargo loads or enforce adherence to load lines. In addition, Lamport and Holt's vessels were managed by an American company that didn't communicate daily operational activities to the home office. Overloading was common, but Lamport and Holt didn't always get away with it. On a number of occasions the owners were reprimanded by the Board of Trade for sending the *Vestris* out overloaded, but despite having been caught repeatedly, the practice continued unabated.

Passenger and cargo liners like the *Vestris* made the bulk of their money by carrying freight. Any revenue from passenger fares was icing on the cake. On this voyage, the *Vestris* would sail with her cargo holds full, making it a very profitable trip, but the amount of human freight on board was a different story. The ship could accommodate 280 passengers in First Class, 180 in Second Class and 200 in Third Class, but as Saturday dawned it became apparent she would depart well below capacity.

Sailing Day brought 128 people from all walks of life—more than enough to keep the crew of nearly 200 busy. As they crossed the gangway, Purser Albert Pugh greeted each passenger and assigned cabins. While he waited to board, First Class passenger Friedrich Puppe stood on the pier watching the stevedores work. He wasn't an expert, but he thought something about the way the cargo was being loaded and stowed didn't look quite right.

Señor Carlos Quiros was concerned for different reasons. He was traveling First Class to Buenos Aires, but before embarking he questioned whether he made a bad choice in travel arrangements. The dapper Chancellor of New York City's Argentine Consulate was going home to visit his mother, but in the circles he ran in, word was out about the *Vestris*. The ship was known for its propensity to list, among other shortcomings. Quiros started having second thoughts when an associate cautioned him the *Vestris* was "the poorest-running boat to South America." Friends ribbed Quiros about his impending demise by telling him to stay close to the life preservers. "Be careful," one warned. "Because the *Vestris* going to meet the *Principessa Mafalda*," referring to the worn-out Italian liner that drowned hundreds when it foundered off the coast of Brazil the year before. Another sent Quiros off with an ominous *Bon Voyage*, "Don't forget what I warned you about the old tub."

Quiros ignored them and became one of two men in diplomatic service bound for the Argentine capital. Japanese army Major Yoshio

"BE CAREFUL WHAT YOU PUT IN THE LOG"

Inouye was en route to assume his assignment as military attaché at his country's embassy. His wife, Teruko was traveling with him. The Inouyes had spent a number of years in Washington, D.C. and counted many U.S. Army officers among their friends.

No movie stars or famous tycoons were aboard, but a few noteworthy names could be found on the passenger list. Sports fans would recognize race car drivers Earl Devore and Norman Batten. The men were the best of friends and the fiercest of competitors. Devore and Batten raced against one another in the Indianapolis 500 twice, with Devore finishing second in 1927 and Batten coming in fifth in May of '28. Devore and his pretty wife, Anne, had enjoyed four fun years of marriage barnstorming the world with their race car, the "Nickel Plate Special" in tow. The couple was traveling from their home in Los Angeles with their wire-haired fox terrier, Speedway Lady. Batten was accompanied by his chestnut-haired wife, Marion. The four were going to South America to race.

The entrepreneurial spirit was also present on board as business travelers sought their fortunes south of the Equator. Tall, dark-haired RCA executive Paul Dana was traveling to Buenos Aires to head up that company's sales office. Oil executive Herbert Johnston and Swiss geologist Dr. Ernst Lehner hoped to discover black gold when they arrived in South America. Clyde Persful, Arthur Jones, Carl Pfaff and Lloyd Ricketts were Oklahoma drillers on their way to Argentina for Standard Oil.

German electrical engineer Friedrich Puppe was taking his wife Charlotte and 7-month-old daughter to his new assignment at a utility in Argentina, but the voyage wasn't starting out as he planned. Immediately after boarding the *Vestris,* Puppe and his family went to their First Class cabin only to discover the majority of their luggage still had yet to arrive. Puppe's steward was also missing, so he went outside and stopped the first one he saw. "I'm not supposed to take care of your cabin," the man told him. "But I will do the best I can to get around to you." Puppe was furious to find out why. "Your steward is too drunk and will be unable to attend to you," the man said. Puppe eventually went looking for his bags on his own and found them mixed in with the trunks and heavy luggage in the cargo hold.

Wyatt Brownfield, 41-year-old chief engineer for the Kentucky Rock Asphalt Company, was assigned to investigate the condition of the roads in Brazil. His 45-year-old wife, Leah, was traveling with him. Leah Brownfield was so afraid of water she even avoided swimming pools, but Wyatt begged her to come along. During thirteen years of marriage the inseparable couple had never been out of the country together and Wyatt believed the trip would provide a great opportunity to reconnect. He pressed his case until Leah relented.

Nevertheless, as the couple became settled in their First Class cabin, all was not well. The superstitious Leah, who had nicknamed her husband "Jinx" years earlier, had a premonition their first voyage would also be their last. At Leah's insistence, on a piece of ship's stationery, the Brownfields listed their assets and wrote out their wills. Wyatt dropped the envelope into the mailbox to be posted before the *Vestris* left port.

Joining them in First Class were 66-year-old William P. Adams and his friend, 72-year-old Dr. August Groman, both of Odebolt, Iowa. Adams was no John Jacob Astor, but he was a millionaire nonetheless, having made his fortune in corn and sheep. He was also a boardroom executive. In addition to having founded and served as president of the First National Bank in Odebolt, Adams was a member of the Board of Directors of International Harvester. His rustic mailing address belied his actual worth. Adams maintained offices in downtown Chicago and owned a mansion in Miami Beach.

In the previous several years, Adams had become a seasoned voyager. He was on the *Vestris* to realize a lifelong dream of fishing off the coast of South America. In addition to his best friend, Adams took his fishing gear and $2,800 cash. Like any adventurer about to take to the jungle might do, he packed a Colt pistol for extra security.

After visiting their five grown children in Tennessee, the Reverend Ernest Alonzo Jackson, his wife, Jannette and 15-year-old son, Cary were headed home to Brazil. The Jacksons were repeat Lamport and

Holt customers, having sailed with the line to South America and back for the previous two decades. Their permanent base was in the U.S., but Ernest and Jannette had spent most of their adult lives in Brazil's interior, spreading the Gospel as Southern Baptist missionaries. In fact, blond-haired, all-American Cary was born in Salvador da Bahia, a coastal city about a thousand miles north of Rio.

Lamport and Holt luggage decal c. 1928.
(*Author's collection*)

Besides being a loving husband and father, 51-year-old E.A., as he was known, was a man of great faith who was fluent in Portuguese. Jackson spoke his adopted language so well he often fooled native speakers. Years before, when some South American ministers began arguing over E.A.'s accent in an effort to pinpoint the Brazilian state he was from, a family friend interrupted to let the incredulous group know how wrong they were. Jackson was born in Glade Spring, Virginia. As E.A. unpacked, 58-year-old Jannette sat down in their First Class cabin with a piece of ship's stationery to pen a quick note to let loved ones know of the family's safe arrival aboard ship. The precocious Cary went up on deck to watch airplanes buzz the Manhattan skyline.

The newlyweds on board included 22-year-old Cline Slaughter and his red-headed 20-year-old bride, Wilma. Slaughter was going on assignment as an auditor for International Harvester so he decided to bring Wilma along for company. Orrin Stevens and Gladys, his wife of three months, were returning to Argentina after a honeymoon in the States. Stevens was going back to his job at the First National Bank of Boston branch in Buenos Aires. He also heard bad things about the *Vestris*, but he didn't give the matter much thought. Stevens figured since it was a British ship it had to be safe.

The Jacksons weren't the only passengers answering to a higher calling. Mormon Church Elders Keith Burt and David Huish were in Second Class on their way to the mission field in Argentina. The trip would mark the first time either had been away from home. After some initial training in Salt Lake City, the young men spent the week exploring Washington, D.C. and New York City. They boarded the *Vestris* exhausted and nearly broke, but they were nevertheless excited to be traveling by ship for the first time in their lives.

Norwegian-born Fredrik Sorensen spent the previous twenty years working as an officer on merchant ships, finally becoming master of his own vessel. However, on this voyage he was content to be just another Second Class passenger. Blond and square-jawed, the 39-year-old had recently been released from the Marine Hospital at Staten Island after undergoing surgery to remove painful varicose veins from his legs. As part of his recovery, Sorensen planned to take advantage of all the warm-water swimming the Barbados had to offer. Sorensen was such an avid swimmer he frequently jumped over the side whenever his ship was stopped and there were a few minutes to spare—much to the delight of his crews.

In Third Class, 29-year-old Gaetano Abbadini and 24-year-old Vincenzo Murri were headed to South America to fetch Abbadini's future wife. After spending years working as a bricklayer in Philadelphia, Abbadini was returning to Buenos Aires to marry Murri's sister. However, the pair almost missed the boat. The previous night's going away party was so intense Abbadini wanted to put off the trip,

"BE CAREFUL WHAT YOU PUT IN THE LOG"

but Murri wouldn't hear anything of it. He poured his hung-over friend onto the Hoboken boat train.

The young men were joined in Third Class by Irish light-heavyweight boxer Harry Fay, who was on his way to Argentina to set up a bout with legendary fighter Luis Angel Firpo, and Jose and Elvira Rua, who were traveling from their home in New Bedford, Connecticut to Brazil to introduce Jose's parents to their grandson, 2-year-old Jorge. The two biggest families aboard the *Vestris* could also be found in Third Class. Jeremiah Alleyne brought his wife and three children: 3-year-old Lillian, 2-year-old Edgeworth and 1-year-old Huntley. Mr. and Mrs. James Headley were traveling with their three girls: 6-year-old Marion, 5-year-old Mildred and 3-year-old Audrey.

Fredrik Sorensen. (*Panorama*)

Rounding out the passenger list was 26-year-old Ovelton Maxey, who was simply trying to get away. Maxey was fleeing a warrant in Virginia for fraudulently obtaining nearly seven thousand dollars worth of loans. Maxey hoped his First Class passage on board the *Vestris* would be his ticket to freedom.

Lamport and Holt literature bragged the ship carried "selected cargo," and that its presence on board kept the vessel "steady in all types of weather." Captain Carey rarely involved himself in discussions related to its loading and stowage, but he found himself in the immediate vicinity of a meeting where some men from the company's shore staff were trying to decide whether an additional two hundred tons of "shut out cargo" could be squeezed in at the last minute. It belonged to firms on the "preference list" of shippers Lamport and Holt didn't want to disappoint, so there was no way it could be left on the pier. The consensus was to bring it aboard immediately. The men looked at the captain. "Very well," he agreed.

At this point, the *Vestris* was so heavy she would have touched bottom, but because the slip had been dredged that summer she remained afloat. It was almost time to go. Second Officer Watson stepped onto the pier to record the ship's draft. He walked fore and aft, looked at the load lines and wrote the measurements down to enter in the ship's log. When he was finished, the 25-year-old made his way back up the gangway to give the numbers to the chief officer.

Frank Johnson had a lot on his plate. One of his new duties required that he write up the crew's lifeboat assignments and give them to Purser Pugh to be typed and posted. His deadline was sometime Sunday or Monday, so there was still plenty of time to finish the list. Besides, crewmen were still signing on while others were jumping ship. The lifeboat assignments would have to wait. The chief officer had more pressing matters to deal with anyway.

Johnson was voyaging with Carey for only the second time, and a lack of communication between the two was already apparent when they met in the chart room. "I've just been around and everything is secure sir," Johnson said. "Be careful what you put in the log about the draft," Carey answered. The captain also mentioned something about putting water in the lifeboats, but Johnson understood what Carey really meant. He would have to report phony numbers regarding the weight of the cargo. The chief didn't argue despite the fact he knew Carey's request was against the law.

"BE CAREFUL WHAT YOU PUT IN THE LOG"

Responsibility for the log entries eventually fell to Second Officer Watson, who was standing nearby and caught bits of the conversation. He wrote the actual draft, twenty-six feet six inches forward and twenty-seven feet eleven inches aft, on a scrap of paper and handed it to Carey. "That's all right," the captain said as he looked at the numbers. "The office will fill in the draft."

Since overloading and fudging paperwork were nothing out of the ordinary, Watson left the space blank where the draft should have been written. He also didn't put anything on the line that specified the total weight of the cargo. Watson signed the form, sent it back to the office and returned to the task of getting the ship ready to shove off. The *Vestris* was loaded nearly a foot below her marks and was legally considered unsafe to take to sea, but no one batted an eyelash.

Loading and coaling had been going on day and night for four days. The stevedores finished their work at 3:30 p.m., giving the crew just fifteen minutes to prepare for what they hoped would be an on-time departure. Carpenter Gus Wohld hung a platform over the side of the ship and caulked and tightened the coaling ports. It was Johnson's job to make sure the work was done correctly, but he didn't have time to check. Wohld climbed back aboard and secured his plank. As gangways were removed and doors secured, the ship's fate was sealed.

On the bridge, Quartermaster Elton Clarke took his place at the wheel and prepared himself for whatever New York Harbor had in store for him. The *Vestris* was one of thirty-three departures that day, and with another twenty-two vessels scheduled to come in, it was always possible to become delayed by traffic congestion in the North River. It had been hours since the *Baltic* and *Scythia* had sailed; the *Vestris* would go out before the *Hamburg*. Tugboats eased the bloated ship out of her berth and nudged her into the river as passengers waved good-bye to friends and loved ones on the pier.

For decades, it had been a Lamport and Holt custom for ship's buglers to play *Auld Lang Syne* as vessels sailed, but it was decided the tune was making passengers feel melancholy about the impending voyage when they should have been getting in a festive mood. The company ultimately issued a directive to save the bugle for meal announcements and pep things up a bit at departure. It worked. Everyone cheered as the orchestra struck up a jazz number. As they played, the *Vestris* steamed slowly past the skyscrapers of New York City, her funnel puffing black smoke into the evening sky. Carey made it out on time.

An advertisement for the *Vestris* and her sisters. (*Author's collection*)

The sun would set in less than an hour. Passengers had nearly twenty-five miles to enjoy the view before the ship reached the open ocean. Some settled into deck chairs to listen to music while others melted away from the rails to explore the interior. Prohibition was in full effect, and with the ship pulling out of "dry" New York, a number of men and women undoubtedly found their way to the bar. After all, 1928 may have been coming to an end, but the twenties were still roaring. Dinner was right around the corner.

A light wind blew in from the northeast as the *Vestris* steamed past the Statue of Liberty. At about 6:00 p.m., the harbor pilot was dropped off at the Ambrose Lightship, and with the sea smooth the *Vestris* set out on the southeasterly course she knew so well. As she did, Baker Thomas Moffatt carried a tall cake out of the galley and set it on a buffet in the First Class dining room. He stayed a moment to admire his work and noticed the cake stood perfectly upright.

Promenade Deck. (*Author's collection*)

Lamport and Holt's red and white house flag flew proudly from the mainmast. It was emblazoned with "L+H" in the middle stripe, with a plus-sign between the letters instead of an ampersand to represent the close friendship of the company's founders. The sentiment was lost on cynical sailors who referred to the flag as the "Lean and Hungry" or the "Lousy and Hungry." However, that's not how passengers were feeling. While they became acquainted with one another over dinner, a tropical storm of epic proportion was forming directly in the ship's path. Meteorological reports identified a wide area of low pressure over the Atlantic Ocean, stretching from the middle of the Eastern Seaboard to the southeast past Bermuda. Ships in that neighborhood were already reporting rotten weather. The *Vestris* would encounter it in just a few hours time.

Far below, dozens of already-filthy firemen tossed their first of thousands of shovelfuls of coal into the fireboxes in an effort to get steam up for the trip. In a world foreign to most of them, Captain Carey stepped away from the bridge to take a nap on the settee in his office with instructions to call him if there was trouble. As he stretched out, Carey may have reflected on the long and successful career he had enjoyed and how it was about to get even better. At the voyage's conclusion he would take command of Lamport and Holt's flagship, the larger and much newer *S.S. Voltaire*. While he dozed, the commodore had no way of knowing that more than a hundred men, women and children in his care had less than forty-eight hours to live.

CHAPTER TWO

"There Is Something the Matter"

As the *Vestris* steamed south on Sunday morning, the weather was getting worse by the minute. The storm's violence didn't allow for ballerina-like grace. Instead, the *Vestris* moved more like a flapper dancing the Charleston. Eighty mile per hour wind gusts battered her port side and whipped up the towering forty foot waves that pounded her mercilessly. Huge clouds of spray blew off the top of the waves and mixed with sheets of rain to drench her decks and everything on them. Due to the wind and water, the *Vestris's* notorious list had returned. The ship was leaning nearly ten degrees to starboard.

In the saloon, Paul Dana and Fred Sorensen were getting to know one another over breakfast. The weather was making it so difficult to get around, the men were two of just a handful of passengers who even bothered to show up. The storm became their main topic of conversation, with Dana remarking it was the worst he had ever seen at sea. Sorensen was a naturalized American, but a hint of a Scandinavian accent came through when he spoke. As the men chatted, Dana found himself so impressed with Sorensen's knowledge of ships he made a mental note to stick close to his new friend on the off chance the situation took a turn for the worse.

The men couldn't have known it, but the *Vestris* was already shipping water in a number of locations. The leaks ranged in size from manageable to severe and engineers were working frantically to stop them. A handful worked in the crew lavatory where water was backing up from the pipes. Others tried to repair the starboard ash ejector. Each time the *Vestris* rolled, the machine known affectionately to firemen as the "Blow George" was blasting so much water into the ship the bilges were nearly full. The machine was supposed to mix firebox ash with water and shoot it out of the ship's hull, but its failure came as no shock. Stokers knew it leaked in rough weather.

The crew also knew both the port and starboard half-doors in the cross-alleyway let water in.[2] It was here crew members battled the most serious leaks they were able to locate. Wohld caulked and tightened the doors repeatedly, but the water would burst out again moments later. The rougher the seas became, the more water would shoot in. Most troubling was where it was going. A series of floor hatches leading to the coal bunkers were left uncovered and thousands of gallons of green seawater poured into the bowels of the ship.

In the engine room, Chief Engineer James Adams had his men rig up pumps in an attempt to get the *Vestris* back on an even keel. Gaining control of the flooding in the cross-alleyway was still a work in progress, but the results of the morning's efforts were encouraging. By midday, Adams reported that both the "Blow George" and the pipes in the crew lavatory had been repaired. It was welcome news, but somewhere there was a much more serious leak that would puzzle Adams, his staff and the ship's officers for the remainder of the voyage. Water was pouring into the stokehold from a coal chute on the

---

[2] The cross-alleyway ran fore and aft through the heart of the ship and was designed to allow firemen to get from the stokehold to their quarters and back without being seen by passengers. The half-doors were two steel doors that opened outward and were used for the loading and unloading of luggage.

"THERE IS SOMETHING THE MATTER"

starboard side at an alarming rate and the coal in the bunkers was becoming saturated. Adams had been an engineer on ships for twenty years, but despite his experience he couldn't figure out how it was getting in.

On the bridge, the storm was severe enough to cause Carey to cancel the second day's customary lifeboat drill. A long blast would have been blown on the ship's siren to alert passengers to go to their boat stations, but it remained silent. There would be no way they could pull it off. As the weather continued to worsen, Watson became concerned. To him, the ship didn't feel alive. The second officer thought the *Vestris* ought to be rising and falling with the waves, but for some reason she wasn't. Watson was suspicious it might have something to do with the amount of cargo on board, but he hoped he was wrong.

In addition, the bloated *Vestris* was handling so badly in the heavy seas it became nearly impossible to keep her on course. The ship's steering problems were also the stuff of legend. It was widely known that even on her best days, the *Vestris* couldn't leave a straight wake. The steering gear was inspected and found to be in good working order, but the old prima donna was performing so badly Carey ordered "all-stop," and the *Vestris* coasted to a halt about two hundred miles east of the Virginia Capes. The captain then commanded the ship be "hove to."[3] Every so often, officers would run the starboard engine in an attempt to point the vessel into the wind, but the engine wasn't powerful enough to move the heavy ship and the tactic didn't work. Instead of slicing through the weather head-on, the *Vestris's* side was left vulnerable to the high winds and broadsides by wave after wave. It was the worst possible position the vessel could be in.

As it had been for Dana and Sorensen, the ship's situation became a topic of curiosity for nearly everyone else. However, because the

---

[3] The *Vestris* wasn't "hove to" in the traditional sense. In this case, the ship was left to lie in the trough of the sea with her helm hard-over and engines stopped. Executed correctly, the tactic would have resulted in the vessel's bow cutting through the waves and weather.

leaks were located in restricted areas, men and women were unaware of the precise state of affairs below decks. Inexperienced voyager Ernst Lehner was unconcerned, chalking the list up to the wind blowing against the *Vestris's* side. Lehner's boss Herbert Johnston disagreed. Johnston had logged thousands of nautical miles in his lifetime, but in this case his experience let him down. "Look here, Lehner. I am glad to see this get going again," he said. "Whenever these people stop a boat there is something the matter." Johnston was way off.

Herbert C.W. Johnston (*David Hurst*)

First Class passenger Edward Marvin also had a feeling something was amiss. He went on deck in an effort to determine whether the ship was still moving. He listened for the sound of the engines. Nothing. He felt for vibration. There was none. He leaned over the rail and looked down at the sea. Marvin's hunch was right. The *Vestris* wasn't making forward progress. She would never do so again.

CHAPTER THREE

"Have You Anything to Communicate?"

The pitching and rocking kept August Groman, Anne Devore and dozens of others laid-up in their cabins for most of the day. By sundown, the storm had reached hurricane proportions. Ship's Surgeon William Sears and Stewardess Clara Ball had their hands full caring for the growing number of seasick passengers.

By contrast, William Wills Davies and his friend Sidney Koppe were feeling fine. Veteran newspaper reporter Davies covered the New York City beat for Argentina's *La Nacion* newspaper while Koppe sold advertisements. The men were planning to attend the same conference in Buenos Aires so they decided to share a First Class cabin. It was turning 6:00 p.m. when Koppe stretched out in his bunk to catch up on some reading. Davies was cracking jokes about the ship's severe rolling when a jet of seawater suddenly blasted through their porthole with a loud crash. The water's force hurled bits of broken glass and strips of wet curtain across the cabin. A stream of water ran down the wall to the floor as the ship creaked and rolled the other direction. When

Davies went to get up, he noticed that a few shards of glass ended up in bed with him.

With their floor awash, Davies called for the steward, who arrived and apologetically began the process of relocating the men to a dry cabin. Johnson and Wohld were next to show up. The chief officer inspected the damage and ordered the carpenter to board up the broken porthole. When Wohld was satisfied his patch would hold, he moved on to other trouble spots.

The news that yet another porthole had given out wasn't a surprise to Johnson, Wohld or anyone else in the crew. It was common knowledge many of them were in such bad shape they were just waiting to break. In Third Class, George doValle's porthole was cracked and leaking so badly his cabin was filling with seawater. Half an inch covered the floor and was starting to spill under his door and into the hallway. doValle's steward tried to repair the porthole himself, but couldn't. At the same time, the portholes in the Second Class ladies bathroom also began to leak.

Over the course of the six months or so he had been aboard, Waiter Thomas Connor had written up dozens of portholes for repair. They were rarely fixed. Connor couldn't figure out why repairs that would have been made immediately on other ships were ignored on the *Vestris*. In reality, because the company was mostly concerned with keeping their ships at sea and full of cargo, proper maintenance fell through the cracks almost by design. Repairs ordered in New York City were referred to Lamport and Holt officials in Argentina, who in turn requested the work be performed in the U.S. In the end, many critical repairs were never made.

The porthole problems marked the beginning of what was to be a rain-soaked evening *inside* the ship, as the dead-in-the-water *Vestris* was punished by the storm. Water poured through ventilators into a handful of Second Class cabins. A wave broke a skylight in the Second Class galley and the ensuing deluge put out the stove's fire, sending a cloud of steam billowing into the smoking room. The hapless cooks were forced to join their counterparts in the First Class galley to finish preparing dinner there.

It was turning 7:00 p.m. As he walked to the bridge for his four-hour shift at the helm, Quartermaster Elton Clarke could feel the ship listing. When he arrived, per captain's orders, he held the wheel all the way to starboard. Clarke stared out the windows at the raging black ocean and reflected on yesterday's departure, when he felt no list at all. High in the crow's nest, the distance Seaman Alexander Crick could see was drastically reduced by the spray coming off the massive waves and the driving rain. Crick hunkered down.

The din of the churning storm was interrupted by the bugle call notifying passengers dinner was about to be served. Because of the problems in the Second Class galley, every passenger regardless of class and all crew members were directed to the First Class saloon. Seating everyone together was such a rare occurrence that 27-year-old Second Steward Alfred Duncan was barely able to reshuffle the table assignments in time.

Everyone could be easily accommodated in the seventy-five foot long dining room, but the prospect of a heavy meal didn't have many takers. Most people were too sick to go down to dinner. Even so, Norman and Marion Batten made an attempt. First Class passengers Edward Walsh, Joseph Twomey and William Burke dined with Purser Albert Pugh. William Wills Davies felt honored to be seated at the captain's table, but for the second night in a row, Carey was nowhere to be seen. Davies was disappointed the captain couldn't make it, but he rightly blamed Carey's absence on the weather.

Carlos Quiros descended the grand staircase into the dining room to find only a handful of daring souls seated at a few lonely tables. The glum atmosphere gave him the excuse he needed. Instead of joining them, Quiros returned to his cabin to order dinner in. Within a few minutes, a steward arrived with his order of broth, eggs and fruit. As Quiros sat down to eat, he began to have an uneasy feeling something was amiss.

LAST DANCE OF THE VESTRIS

The British Marconi Company provided the *Vestris* with three wireless operators, and the young men exemplified the best the British Isles had to offer. Off-duty Chief Operator Michael O'Loughlin of County Wexford, Ireland and his number two, James MacDonald of Banff, Scotland went down to dinner, leaving Londoner Charles Verchere alone in the wireless room. Where Quiros was disappointed to see so few passengers in the saloon, MacDonald was cheered by what he thought were so many. He guessed more of them would have been relegated to their cabins.

First Class saloon. (*Author's collection*)

On board Lamport and Holt liners, dinner was a grand affair. Passengers enjoyed elaborate meals while a small orchestra serenaded them with marches, waltzes and popular selections. Typical fare included Hors d'oeuvres, followed by a hot or cold soup and an entrée. Haunch of mutton with red currant jelly, prime rib au jus, roast gosling with orange compote, roast partridge and boiled salmon with cucumber in Hollandaise sauce were often on the menu. The old English standby of lamb with mint sauce also appeared frequently. Dinner was typically followed by a rich dessert of plum pudding with brandy sauce or ice cream, all of it brought out on Lamport and Holt's green and gold monogrammed china service.

The ship shuddered as it rode to the crest of each wave before plunging back down again, making eating an extremely challenging task. Woodwork creaked. In an effort to prevent china from sliding off the tables, waiters poured water on tablecloths to try and get plates and bowls to stick in place. Even so, nearly everyone had to use a free hand to hold on to sliding china. MacDonald purposely stayed away from the soup, yet still struggled with his fish. Sorensen found it difficult to keep pace with all the courses so he finally asked his waiter to bring everything out on the same plate.

Another view of the First Class saloon. The grand staircase can be seen in the background. (*Author's collection*)

While dinner continued in the saloon, music could be heard coming from one of the cabins along the Second Class hallway. Mormon missionaries Keith Burt and David Huish skipped their meals and were passing the time by staging an impromptu concert. Huish sang and played the harmonica while Burt blew on his saxophone, but they weren't having much fun. Since leaving New York, both young men had been seasick and spent most of the day in their bunks trying to avoid any more vomiting. The two decided to call it a night when Burt became tired of wrangling with some broken sax keys. Huish put the cabin light out and the young men went to sleep.

Half an hour had passed since dinner began. High above the deck, Lookout Crick peered out at the sea and saw something highly unusual and extremely disturbing. Two massive black waves had formed off the port bow and were headed straight for the ship. Even from the crow's nest, they looked as high as a tall building. Crick didn't have time to warn the captain. He braced himself for impact. On the bridge, Third Officer Welland saw the waves loom up ominously directly in front of the ship. There was nothing he could do. A fraction of a second later, the waves struck the *Vestris* in quick succession. The ship lurched instantly to starboard and quivered from end to end. Quartermaster Clarke felt the wheel give a sudden jerk and watched the sea surge up to the bridge windows.

Terrified passengers heard a tremendous crash and felt two nearly simultaneous blows, with the first being larger than the second. In a split second, everything that wasn't bolted down was hurled to the starboard side of the ship. In the dining room, people and chairs went flying in all directions. Dinner came to an abrupt end as china, glasses and cutlery went flipping off tables and crashing to the floor. One waiter tripped over a passenger's shoulder, landed in the center of the table and rolled off. The top of William Burke's table became detached from its base and took off across the room. He tried to dodge it, but the table smashed into his face as it zoomed past, leaving him dazed and his jaw bleeding. Burke ended up in the corner with his table mates and their dinners piled on top of him.

The *Vestris* shook violently for nearly a minute. Second Marconi Operator MacDonald thought it felt like the ship moved as if on a giant corkscrew. Making the scene even more surreal, there was no screaming.

In his cabin, Carlos Quiros saw his wristwatch fly off the nightstand as he tumbled across the room along with furniture, luggage and half-eaten bits of food. From the floor, he watched a bunk tear away from the wall.

Even the wireless room on the roof of the Verandah Café wasn't immune from the violence. Third Operator Verchere had his headset ripped off when he was thrown out of his chair. Seawater squirted through the cracks of the door and something heavy slammed against the wall. The terrified 18-year-old was sure it was a piece of mast.

Quartermaster Lionel Licorish was sleeping when he suddenly felt himself flying across the room. In No. 1 cargo hold, the three crated Chevrolets broke through a wooden wall with a deafening crash. The cars slid fifteen feet to starboard and ended up in the crew's quarters. Licorish was buried beneath a pile of debris, but uninjured. He freed himself and ran to see what happened. In the storeroom, George Amsdell was knocked to the floor. To him, it felt like the *Vestris* rose out of the sea and dropped back down. Amsdell went to investigate what he believed was surely a collision.

Adams and his men felt the ship's convulsions in the engine room. Sixth Engineer Reginald Dickson was in the alleyway between the stokehold and the engine room when the waves struck. He thought it felt like going up in an elevator and coming down with a hard bump. Fourth Engineer George Prestwich was working on the ash ejector valve when, to his horror, he looked up and saw a wave of green seawater coming his way. Prestwich was knocked down. He stood up in time to hear an avalanche of coal fall inside the bunker.

Only tablecloths remained on the dining room tables. Shards of broken china, cutlery and food covered the floor. The silence was broken when some of the women began sobbing softly as they stood up to leave. More than a dozen people hobbled toward the surgery to seek treatment for a variety of bumps, bruises and cuts. In an effort to keep passengers from becoming truly alarmed, Johnson, Bolger and

Watson stuck around and played it cool for a few minutes before casually departing for the bridge. To Watson, it felt like something pushed the ship over. He observed that in most cases, when a vessel labors in a heavy sea and a wave strikes her, "she shakes and comes back again." The *Vestris* did not.

Damage reports began to come in from locations throughout the ship. Two lifeboats were knocked off their chocks and some deck railing was carried away. The Second Class smoking room was flooded. In the abandoned Second Class dining room, water poured in from yet another broken skylight, leaving a foot of it sloshing around on the floor. Additional portholes were reported leaking. Cook John Henry Burn's dresser was afloat in his quarters. Baggage Master William MacDonald found nearly two feet of water in his room. Herman Rueckert returned to his First Class cabin to find his luggage floating around. Stewards relocated him to another cabin, but when it also filled with water, Rueckert was moved a second time.

Carlos Quiros threw on a pair of trousers and went to see what happened. He soon ran into an officer who told him everything was OK and to go back to his cabin, which he did. Quiros's thoughts again turned to food, so he called his steward and ordered fruit and champagne. The man eventually delivered something close: a gin-and-tonic and some grapes. He apologized, telling Quiros the kitchen and bar were too much of a mess to fill the order precisely. Quiros ate and drank, then drifted off to sleep.

"Sparks" O'Loughlin and MacDonald returned to the wireless room where the sore-eared Verchere told them what happened to him when the waves hit. The third operator was making his first trip aboard the *Vestris* and had only been on the job a total of three months when he was rag-dolled across the room. Of the three, MacDonald had been at sea the longest, thirteen years; the quiet and meticulous O'Loughlin had eleven under his belt. As the listing *Vestris* pitched and her passengers nursed injuries and vomited, the operators resumed their usual routine.

"HAVE YOU ANYTHING TO COMMUNICATE?"

MUSICAL PROGRAMME
1. March "The Masquerade"
2. Waltz "Beautiful Blue Danube"
3. "Temple Bells"
4. Selection "Naughty Marietta"
5. "Kashmiri Song"

MENU

T.S.S. "VESTRIS."
Sunday, April 29th, 1928.

DINNER

Consomme Fleuri.   Creme Francaise.

Boiled Salmon, Cucumber, Hollandaise Sauce.

Calves Sweetbreads, Epinards.

Prime Ribs and Sirloin of Beef au Jus.

Garden Turnips.

Boiled & Browned Potatoes.

Roast Gosling, Orange Compote.

Plum Pudding, Hard & Brandy Sauce.

Bavaroise au Caramel.

Ice Cream and Wafers.

Cheese.   Dessert.   Coffee.

A *Vestris* souvenir menu from 1928. The ship would sink six months and two weeks after this meal was served. (*Author's collection*)

LAST DANCE OF THE VESTRIS

It wasn't long before they received a message from the *Voltaire*. The running mates were due to pass one another sometime Monday, but the *Voltaire* was running behind, delayed by the storm and a broken propeller. Her operators had tried raising the *Vestris* on a number of occasions that day, but the older ship did not answer. According to procedure, the Marconi men couldn't respond without permission from the bridge. Just before 9:00 p.m., the *Voltaire* tried again, sending QRU.[4] Although enough had happened for the *Vestris's* operators to have transmitted a novel, they didn't answer. MacDonald went to bed to catch a few hours sleep before his watch.

In their First Class cabin, Cline and Wilma Slaughter slept soundly. Remarkably, the newlyweds were undisturbed by the storm, the crash or the waves.

---

[4] QRU was the wireless code for "Have you anything to communicate?" Sending QRU in response indicated "We have nothing to communicate."

CHAPTER FOUR

"The Ship is Sinking, but Very Slowly"

The waves' impact instantly gave the *Vestris* a starboard list of nearly twenty degrees. The ship was now leaning over so dramatically she was lying on her leaky half-doors, causing jets of seawater to blast through the cracks into the cross-alleyway.

Crew members reacted quickly to combat the sudden inrush of water that seemed to be coming from everywhere. Johnson worked to stop up a broken porthole in the firemen's quarters. The sea was also hissing in through the portholes in the stewards' lavatory. Storekeeper George Amsdell tried to tighten the screws, but there were no nuts. When he returned with the necessary hardware, Amsdell discovered the screws were so thick with coats of paint the nuts couldn't be threaded. Carpenter Wohld was busy running around trying to fix as many broken portholes as he could. Somehow he also found the time to venture outside to inspect the lifeboats that were knocked out of their chocks. They escaped damage.

What the crew didn't know was that the ship was mortally wounded. Carey would have been justified in having "Sparks" send an

SOS, but he chose not to. Consequently, in the wireless room it was still business as usual. At midnight, Verchere woke MacDonald so he could receive the next day's news stories for publication in the ship's newspaper. MacDonald was making his first trip on the *Vestris,* but the process of "taking the press" was the same on every liner.

As he began his shift, the Marconi office was beginning to resemble a funhouse. Despite the difficulties inherent to the increasingly bad angle, MacDonald wasn't alarmed. The bespectacled 34-year-old made the best of his situation by using a stack of books to prop up the typewriter. Dots and dashes filled MacDonald's ears with the details of President-elect Hoover's trip to the Deep South, a speculative frenzy overwhelming Wall Street and other stories. For the next few hours, MacDonald would focus on ensuring passengers would have their news at breakfast.

After the dinnertime disaster, Paul Dana and Fred Sorensen met up and headed to the smoking room for a few drinks and a review of the night's events. Most of the furniture had slid across to the starboard side of the room, so Dana and Sorensen grabbed a pair of chairs, wedged them against a wall and resumed the conversation they began at breakfast. They picked a good location. From where the men were sitting, they could reach around a wall to grab their whiskey-and-sodas directly from the bartender. After a few hours of conversation, Dana excused himself and went off to bed. He pushed his bunk into a corner to keep it from sliding around, climbed in and closed his eyes.

Dr. Lehner made his way to the Verandah Café and sat down at a table near honeymooners Orrin and Gladys Stevens. The café was mostly deserted, with just a few other passengers huddled together on the other side of the room. Consequently, he couldn't help but overhear the young couple's conversation. Orrin was desperately trying to soothe his terrified bride, but getting through to her was proving to be difficult. Gladys's mind was made up—the *Vestris* and everyone aboard her were doomed. The geologist joined them in an effort to help Orrin explain that everything would be alright. It was a good thing he did. Lehner's words seemed to calm Gladys and he excused himself at 9:00 p.m. The geologist was sleeping soundly a few hours later when

"THE SHIP IS SINKING, BUT VERY SLOWLY"

he was awakened by the voice of a man outside his cabin door. "Well she isn't any worse than she was four hours ago," was all Lehner could make out. He rolled over and went back to sleep.

Orrin Stevens passport photo. (*National Archives/Mike Poirier*)

Fred Puppe's eyes opened at 2:00 a.m. when he thought he heard the engines stop. Adding to his suspicion was the fact he felt no vibration. Charlotte woke up with a start and told him she was worried about the baby. "We are in safe hands," Puppe told her. "There is something wrong but the captain knows. He will take care of it. The ship is sinking, but very slowly. Don't be afraid." Puppe went on to explain that a dozen rescue ships would be on scene long before they would ever be needed. Despite the fact he revealed his belief the ship would founder, the pep talk worked. Satisfied with her husband's explanation, Charlotte went back to sleep.

Isaac Scott only wished he could. The restless steward made his way to the pantry for a cup of coffee, but there wasn't enough steam to make any, as every available ounce was being used to run the pumps. Frustrated, Scott lay down on the deck and closed his eyes. Far below in the engine room, an exhausted Chief Engineer Adams sat down to a cup of cold coffee and a sandwich.

CHAPTER FIVE

"Don't Take Time to Shave"

By 4:00 a.m. the situation had become so serious there was no going back. No matter what measures officers and crew took to avoid it, the *Vestris* would eventually sink. Unfortunately, Carey couldn't read the handwriting on the wall. Instead, as the storm showed signs of dying down, the captain began to believe his ship could be *saved*.

Below decks, seawater was coming in along the engine room walls in sheets. Under ideal conditions, the ship's three pumps could remove two thousand tons of water an hour, but they weren't getting the job done. The pumps were so badly clogged with coal dust and bits of coal they could only manage a fraction of their normal capacity. It was also beginning to look doubtful the firemen could maintain the steam needed to keep the pumps going at all. As the water gained, it became obvious the machines had failed.

From the bridge, the increasingly befuddled captain was trying to pinpoint the exact location the water was entering the ship. He considered the coaling ports. Carpenter Wohld insisted he secured them tightly, but Carey wondered if one or more were wrenched open while the ship strained in the storm. The captain also considered the possibility a scupper plate had come off and the opening was letting water in. Both were unlikely, but Carey had to find out quickly. He dispatched Watson to the engine room to confer with Adams and sent Johnson and 23-year-old Third Officer Welland below to inspect the coal bunkers.

Watson was first to return. He conveyed the chief engineer's assessment that the inflow was under control and the water in the bilges was beginning to subside. Watson passed the news to the captain despite the fact he felt it was entirely too optimistic and the opposite was probably occurring. Carey was puzzled. "Well," he wondered aloud. "If they are controlling the water and it has gone down a foot, what is still increasing our list?"

In the flooded cross-alleyway, Johnson and Welland could hear water running inside the coal bunkers. The men went back to the bridge with their intelligence. "It's bad," Welland told Carey. "The situation is serious," the captain agreed. "Undoubtedly we are taking water somewhere else. Somewhere we do not know about." Carey decided to go below with Johnson to listen for himself. When the men reached the cross-alleyway, the water was all the way up to the porthole in the half-door. Carey and his chief officer waded in and placed their heads against the bulkhead. Hearing the sound of rushing water moved the captain to hand down his first in a series of absurd orders. "Go muster all hands, set them to bailing and report back to me," Carey told Johnson. Incredibly, despite the fact the ship and everyone aboard her were in grave danger, Carey and his chief officer wouldn't speak again for another six hours.

Johnson and Welland went to the crew's quarters, gathered up about sixty men, including all the stewards and about a dozen off-duty firemen, and ordered them to grab pails and go to the cross-alleyway to begin bailing out the ship. The men weren't exactly thrilled with the assignment. Second Steward Duncan thought it was a dumb idea, but he and everyone else obeyed without question. Under the command of Storekeeper Amsdell, the men formed a bucket brigade in front of the half-doors, scooping up water black with coal dust and passing it upstairs to the deck where it was dumped over the side. A crewman later jokingly described the group as being "a few buckets against the Atlantic."

Johnson didn't think the bailers would make much of a difference, but he agreed with the captain—the ship might still have a chance if the weather continued to abate. The chief officer understood the peril the *Vestris* was in, but like Watson he chose not to press the issue with Carey. Nor did he suggest sending an SOS. Johnson left the matter of what to do up to the captain.

It was a critical juncture. Carey should have used the pumps' failure as his excuse to ask for help. 4:00 a.m. also marked the last moment a distress call could have been sent to be effective. If Carey had a good reason for not sending one he never explained it to his officers. Instead, he kept his thoughts to himself. The captain had a lot on his mind. While he directed the increasingly ridiculous measures he hoped would save the ship, Carey was weighed down by the additional pressures of everything ranging from company policy to public perception. Orders for a captain in his predicament were spelled out in Lamport and Holt's operations manual, *General Instructions to Masters:*

> In the event of a serious disaster happening to one of the vessels of this line at sea, the master must in the first instance calmly consider the actual amount of peril there may be to the lives of those under his charge, and then judge if he will be justified in fighting his own way unaided to the nearest port. His being able to succeed in this will always be considered as a matter of high recommendation to him as a master.

By law, the owners of vessels in distress were liable for salvage fees—the costs incurred by rescue ships. In the *Vestris's* case, the total amount would be in the hundreds of thousands of dollars, with Lamport and Holt reluctantly footing the bill. Whether Carey believed his company's directive to be a businessman's guideline for avoiding huge payouts or a seaman's blueprint for saving lives, he would obey it. Even in the absence of what would later be known as The Order that

"DON'T TAKE TIME TO SHAVE"

Should Not Stand, Carey, a savvy captain with decades of experience, would never have elected to send SOS or abandon ship if there existed the slightest chance of saving his vessel, anyway.

Besides salvage fees, Carey also knew the negative publicity stirred up by an unnecessary distress call would damage Lamport and Holt's good name. Choosing to fight his own way to the nearest port meant the company would get to keep their money and the commodore would almost certainly get to keep his job.

Most importantly, Carey had the passengers' safety to consider. All he had to do was look over the side to see that the seas were still menacingly high. The captain knew the eighteen-foot waves would make quick work of the thirty-foot-long lifeboats and drown every last man, woman and child aboard them. Conversely, a vessel as large as the *Vestris* had no problem with swells of that size. Carey decided the safest place for everyone was on the ship—for now.

Like Watson, the captain may have believed Adams's assessment of the situation to be too rosy, because he went to the engine room to confer with his chief engineer personally. As the two spoke, Carey couldn't help but notice the rivers of seawater pouring in from above. He asked Adams if anything could be done to stem the flow. The chief finally came clean and revealed the disturbing truth: the *Vestris* was letting water in faster than it could be pumped out. Despite the news, Carey was still hopeful. He glanced at a blackboard hanging on a wall nearby. Written on it were the words "Starboard No. 4 and 5 emptied." The captain had previously ordered the two ballast tanks pumped out in an effort to correct the list. Thus far, it hadn't worked. He took another look around and ordered Adams to pump out starboard tank No. 2. "That should bring her up," he said. With that, Carey went back to the bridge.

Engineers set the pump to work as the captain instructed, but with each stroke the list actually became worse. The ship's lower half was being lightened as the tank was pumped out, while the upper half, made increasingly more top-heavy with the weight of the saturated coal in the bunkers, was pulling the vessel over. The concept was lost on Carey and Adams. The captain's order and the chief engineer's failure to recognize its consequences served only to shorten the lives of the vessel and scores of passengers and crew aboard her.

At about the same time, Third Officer Welland finally got around to giving the Marconi men the go-ahead to reply to the *Voltaire*'s most recent inquiry. Incredibly, he ordered them to tell the other liner they had nothing to report. Within moments, the QRU signal was sent and the *Vestris's* struggle for life remained a secret.

(Panorama graphic)

After hours of work and thousands of bucketsful of water, it became clear to the bailers their exertions weren't helping to correct the list. First Class passenger Edward Walcott was in his cabin when he overheard a conversation between two crewmen. "Aren't you going down to bail?" one asked the other. "It is useless bailing anymore," was the reply. "The ship cannot survive."

By dawn, the *Vestris* was listing nearly thirty degrees to starboard and passengers were waking up to the reality they were on a sinking ship. Others didn't have to wake up at all. Herbert Johnston spent a sleepless night in the smoking room. He rightly estimated the *Vestris* had been in serious trouble since about midnight and her time was running short. With his mind made up as to the ship's future, Johnston decided to take steps to ensure he and his friends would survive when she sank. He returned to his cabin and put on a second pair of trousers, two vests and pulled a pair of golf stockings on over his socks. As he rushed out, Johnston grabbed his valuables and jammed them into his pockets.

Dr. Lehner was the first to be roused when Johnston barged into his cabin at 6:00 a.m. "Lehner, I think you are very much safer on deck," he said. "You had better get up and get dressed." In direct contrast to Johnston, Lehner had passed a pleasant night. "I am sleeping here quite comfortably, thank you," he said before rolling over and closing his eyes. Undeterred, his boss moved on, visiting the cabins of Walcott and others to urge them to dress quickly and get on deck.

A worried William Adams went to get his friend August Groman. Weak and exhausted from a sleepless night battling seasickness, he could barely get out of bed. Dr. Groman hadn't had anything to eat in the previous twenty-four hours, so he called for his steward and asked for some grapefruit. "I'm afraid, sir, I can't get you any grapefruit," the steward said with a look of concern on his face. "Nearly all the food has been ruined by the storm."

"Then get me some other kind of fruit. I don't care what it is."

"I'll do the best I can, sir."

The steward stepped out as Groman began to dress. The doctor's clothing was hanging high and dry on a hook, but his shoes were a different story. He found them afloat on the cabin floor. Half an hour later, the steward returned with a handful of grapes. His look of concern had given way to one of dismay. When Groman asked him what was happening to the ship, the steward's eyes welled up and he began to cry. "I'm sorry, sir, but I can say nothing," he sobbed. "Orders are orders. I can't talk. God, I'd like to tell you, but I think you know what I am trying to say." With that, the man turned and left the cabin. Groman never saw him again.

Johnston, Edward Walcott and Orrin Stevens met in the smoking room. "I think we ought to go and ask the captain what the devil is the matter," Johnston argued. It was a tough sell. Walcott countered that bothering the captain was unnecessary, saying Carey obviously knew the ship was in danger. A groggy and perturbed Dr. Lehner joined them in time to hear Walcott conclude that it would be unfair to further burden the captain. "He knows his job. He will take care of us," Lehner agreed. Johnston gave up the idea and stepped outside alone. As he walked along the boat deck, he passed a handful of stewards. Johnston was sure he heard one of them say the ship was finished.

First Class cabin. (*Author's collection*)

Meanwhile, Carey was again in conference with Adams, who had ventured topside with bad news. The chief engineer told the captain that No. 2 tank had been pumped dry with no benefit. "She doesn't seem to come up any," Adams said. Carey agreed, "I am afraid she hasn't." Adams told the captain the pumps were now at work emptying the bilges. The news gave Carey hope, but he was grasping at straws. "Keep going," he ordered.

When William Wills Davies woke up, he looked out his starboard "Bibby" porthole. What he saw reminded him of looking down a deep well. First Class passenger Edward Johnson made a similar discovery after being awakened by something pounding against his cabin wall. When he went to investigate, Johnson learned it was actually the sound of waves banging into the side of the ship. He was alarmed at how

"DON'T TAKE TIME TO SHAVE"

close the water had come up to his porthole during the night and decided it could do double duty as a sink. Johnston figured if he wanted to wash his hands in the ocean, all he would have to do was open the porthole and stick them outside.[5]

The Devores' cabin offered the couple a similar view and Anne became especially alarmed. Her husband's observation couldn't have helped matters. "I have never been on a ship where there has been such a serious list," Earl Devore said as he peered out the porthole. "It looks to me like serious trouble." It was at that moment Norman Batten entered and urged his friends to hurry up and get on deck. "Don't take time to shave," he warned.

---

[5] The *Vestris* featured "tandem cabins," which were designed to give passengers with inside staterooms access to light and fresh air in the form of a porthole at the end of a narrow hallway. Belfast shipbuilder Harland and Wolff pioneered the design for Liverpool's Bibby Line in 1902.

CHAPTER SIX

"Get Up, Charlie, This is Serious"

Ordinarily, breakfast on the *Vestris* was served promptly at 8:30 a.m., but on this morning nothing was offered. Besides the challenges inherent to preparing food on a severely listing ship, so much seawater had come up through the garbage chute the kitchen was closed and abandoned.

For Fred Puppe and nearly everyone else, "Lean and Hungry" had become a reality. Having had nothing but bad luck with stewards the entire voyage, he now found himself alone in the saloon foraging for a bite to eat. The portholes were closed, but as each wave drilled the ship's side, jets of seawater shot into the room through their rotten gaskets. The effect made the wall look like a fountain. Puppe figured the scene was probably repeating itself below decks, and consequently the ship was in more serious trouble than he originally believed. To top it off, his was a wasted errand. There was no coffee, tea or even water to drink, but someone *did* leave out bunches of bananas. Puppe grabbed a couple and returned to his cabin, where he found Charlotte so seasick she couldn't get out of her bunk. He took the lead in caring for the equally sick baby Lisolette, feeding the famished infant some crushed up bananas.

The scene in the dining room made enough of an impression on Puppe that he decided to get his family up to the lifeboats as quickly as possible, despite their seasickness. He ripped the leather straps off his suitcases and fastened them snugly around Charlotte so he could pull her along the sloping decks more easily. The little family exited the cabin and made their way up the stairs. When the Puppes reached the smoking room they took a seat on the floor and wedged themselves against a wall to wait for instructions. They joined dozens of others who were doing the same.

Mormon missionaries Keith Burt and David Huish said their morning prayers and headed out to get something to eat. It had become nearly impossible to walk down the tilted hallways without falling down. The landlubbers made progress only by gripping their way along the handrails. In the saloon they found people either milling about or sitting on the floor. None were eating breakfast. Huish was given an earful when he asked a fellow passenger where the stewards were. "They're all down in the coal bunkers bailing out water," the man said. "Wouldn't you rather go without your breakfast than lose your life?" He was wrong about the location, but the sentiment was dead on.

It was at this moment the young men realized they were in mortal danger. "This is getting to be a serious matter," Burt said to Huish. "Something is dreadfully wrong." Their appetites now a thing of the past, the two made their way aft to the smoking room to eavesdrop on conversations there. Burt and Huish heard one man swear an SOS had been sent, but was canceled because the captain thought the crew could save the ship. Another group discussed the severity of the list, while still others argued over whether the *Vestris* was even moving. In any case, the young men, feeling seasick and discouraged, went back to their cabin where they quickly discovered they could hardly lie down without rolling out of their bunks.

Dr. Groman left his cabin to begin his journey to the boat deck. It was much slower going for the seasick 72-year-old than it had been for the young missionaries. In his weakened condition, he could hardly walk. When Groman reached for the handrail to steady himself for the climb up a flight of stairs, his arm gave out suddenly and he dropped headfirst into the flooded stairwell below, banging his head on the way down. No one saw him fall. The soaked and dazed physician would have to climb out alone.

Fred Sorensen was just waking up. He rolled over, fell out of his bunk and hit the floor with a thud. He hadn't expected the list to be so serious. Sorensen threw on a sweater and some khaki trousers and went to take a look around. In the dining room, he came upon the meager breakfast of bananas. Sorensen took a few bunches to hand out to other passengers on his way to his second stop, the smoking room. Once there, he surveyed the scene for a few minutes but didn't stay, opting instead to go back for more bananas.

As Sorensen negotiated the staircase leading to the glass-domed entrance hall, he heard cries for help. Upon further investigation, he discovered that a passenger had slipped, tumbled along the floor and crashed through a door leading outside to the starboard promenade deck. The railing was acting as a basket of sorts, preventing the man from washing out to sea. However, as Sorensen crept closer, he saw not one, but three people hanging on for their lives. Two stewards had fallen out while trying to get to the man, but with the rail under water and the treacherous incline of the deck, they couldn't climb back up. Sorensen found himself energized. Although his legs weren't completely healed, he crawled down to the men and stretched out his hand. One of the stewards had a nasty cut on his wrist that smeared blood all over Sorensen as he was pulled to safety. The other was bleeding from his nose. After much straining, Sorensen and the stewards were able to get the man back on board.

Paul Dana looked out his porthole and couldn't see the horizon. Things hadn't improved overnight as he had hoped. What was worse, seawater was sloshing on his cabin floor. As Dana gathered his thoughts, his steward came in complaining of a sore shoulder. He told Dana about his night spent bailing and left him a banana. Dana ate it while he dressed and exited to make his way up to the boat deck.

"GET UP, CHARLIE, THIS IS SERIOUS"

By this time, officers realized the bailing party had failed and the pumping out of the ballast tanks had only made things worse. A worn-out Captain Carey finally came to the conclusion the *Vestris* needed help. He summoned First Officer Bolger to the bridge and asked him to determine the ship's position. The 27-year-old had difficulties because the ship was too far from shore for the radio direction finder to be effective, so Carey calculated them himself by dead reckoning. He marked the position on a chart. "Get a message over to all ships in the vicinity to stand by if necessary," he ordered Bolger. The first officer rushed to the wireless room to relay the order to O'Loughlin. Second Operator MacDonald had been asleep about four hours when he was awakened by excited conversation between the two. He woke Verchere with a shake, "Get up, Charlie, this is serious."

The wireless signal CQ put ships and shore stations on alert, only. Any vessel receiving the call wouldn't change course or begin rescue operations. Instead, ships within earshot would monitor the situation in the event a full-blown distress signal followed. In addition, if an operator preparing to sign off heard CQ, he would remain on duty in order to listen in. According to procedure, if the danger passed the call would be canceled. O'Loughlin sent the signal, along with the message: "We are heeling over and may need assistance. Please broadcast the following to all ships and stations: Keep close watch for distress calls from *S.S. Vestris*, who may need immediate help." Within a few minutes, Joseph Finzimer, the operator at the coastal wireless station at Tuckerton, New Jersey had rebroadcast the message. The *Vestris* had been doomed since four o'clock that morning. It was now nearly twenty minutes to nine.

Ever the newshound, reporter Davies decided to write a story about the *Vestris's* plight and transmit it to *La Nacion*. He penned a quick message to Carey to see if he would answer a few questions. Predictably, the captain declined. Undeterred, Davies decided to pay a visit to the wireless room anyway. He stuck his head in the doorway and, after explaining that he was a reporter, asked if he could join them for awhile. They agreed, so Davies sat on the floor and wedged his legs against a table to watch them work.

CHAPTER SEVEN

"Stay with Me, I'm Going to Live"

By mid-morning, the storm that had tormented the *Vestris* was but a memory. The sun shone brightly through puffy white clouds and the once tempestuous seas had calmed greatly. Unfortunately, there was no respite in the stokehold, where Chief Engineer Adams was pleading with his firemen for more steam. He telephoned the captain and asked for permission to shut down the port engine—with the intention of using the additional steam for the pumps. Carey gave him the go-ahead. Within moments the pumps were working faster, but the captain knew it was probably too little, too late.

With each additional inch the *Vestris* heeled over, the more passengers and crew were coming to the conclusion she was done for. Pantryman Alfred Hanson was one. The 27-year-old was already a veteran mariner; he had spent his entire adult life on ships, including a four year stint in the Swedish navy. Having just finished bailing with the others, he went below to get his life belt. He also grabbed his camera. Hanson appeared on deck to shoot a few photographs of the badly-listing liner. He took a couple of quick shots from the aft cargo hatch looking forward before moving to the port side rail. Once there, he turned, looked forward and snapped two more. Hanson used two more exposures before putting his camera away to join some other exhausted stewards in their search for a bite to eat.

In this Fred Hanson photograph, the *Vestris* is listing more than thirty degrees to starboard. (*Wide World*)

Carlos Quiros awoke after enduring a miserable night. He rose with an unquenched thirst for champagne and called for his steward. This time the man was unable to deliver a thing. Instead, he started to make up the bed while Quiros dressed. The diplomat left him a ten dollar tip before stepping out.

When Quiros arrived on deck, he joined Paul Dana and a handful of others watching incredulously as the second officer and some crew members worked to jettison cargo in a last-ditch attempt to correct the list. Because every ounce of steam was being used to run the pumps, the deck cranes were off and the work was being done by hand. Quiros watched as the men opened a cargo hatch and began heaving meat chains and heavy boxes out, sliding them down the deck and over the side, where they hit the water with great splashes. The operation didn't exactly convey a sense of security to the group of passengers looking on. A grinning man muttered to no one in particular, "Well anyway, we've got a nice day to be wrecked on."

Officers also determined the three Chevrolets had to go. After much straining and effort, crewmen managed to get one of them out of a hatch and over the side into the sea. They began work on another, but it became stuck on the rail. No amount of pushing or pulling could dislodge the second car from its perch. Freeing it was a lost cause, so Watson left for the bridge to tell Carey there was no point in continuing to try. The Chevy was eventually abandoned where it was—hanging halfway over the ship's side.

Paul Dana averted his eyes from the excitement to see a cheerful-looking officer brush by a group of passengers and answer their questions with the morning's boilerplate answer to queries about the ship's situation, "Not to worry." However, Dana *was* worried. He knew time was running out, so he decided to make the now-treacherous trip back to retrieve the cash he'd hidden in his room. He ran down the stairway that led to the First Class cabins and was horrified to see the hallway below him filling with warm Gulf Stream seawater. Dana waded to his cabin. Once there, he made yet another disturbing discovery. The trunk containing his money was underwater and wedged firmly underneath the bunk. With the water rising, Dana tugged and pulled, but it wouldn't budge. He finally gave up the trunk and its contents, satisfied to make it out of the creaky cabin alive. Dana stuffed his passport and a pack of cigarettes into his pocket and sloshed his way back to the boat deck.

Carlos Quiros stopped Second Steward Duncan as he rushed past. "Listen, I'm not a captain or anything like that, but I'm pretty sure this ship won't survive another roll," he observed. Duncan told him not to worry and hastily excused himself. As Duncan hurried away, Quiros watched a group of women stop him further down the deck. Undoubtedly, their question was along the same lines and undoubtedly, the second steward gave the same answer. Quiros next tried approaching the captain for an explanation. "No danger at all," Carey told him. "We shall have this trouble over very soon, then everything will be all right." Quiros didn't believe it, so he grabbed a life belt and began to put it on under his coat. Doing so opened him up to ridicule from a few people who were watching him tie the straps. "You won't need a life preserver," one shouted. "The captain told us so."

Carlos Quiros. (Wide World)

"If you are wise you will go and get them right now," Quiros shot back. "I believe you'll need them soon and by then it might be too late."

While eyeing the passengers standing along the rail, Quiros noticed the familiar face of a forlorn-looking Spaniard. He recognized him because the man recently visited the consulate to obtain a visa. Quiros initially denied the request, but when the man explained he had a family in the U.S. and was only going to Argentina for a short visit, Quiros relented. At the time, the man was ecstatic. Now he looked dejected. The wry Quiros called out to him, "Aren't you sorry I gave you that visa?" He didn't answer. Quiros moved on and ran into his friend William Wills Davies, fresh from his stint in the wireless room. The two discussed the inevitable. "Stay with me," Quiros said. "I'm going to live." Davies asked him why. "Because of my mother," he said.

Despite the storm, the lurch and the list, newlyweds Cline and Wilma Slaughter enjoyed a very sound night's sleep and were still dozing lazily in their beds. Cline rolled over and opened his eyes to see a coat hanging on the hook in their cabin sticking straight out of the wall. It was enough to motivate him to go outside to find out what was happening. Slaughter fumbled on the sloping floor as he dressed, but he took his time just the same. He had no idea they were in such danger.

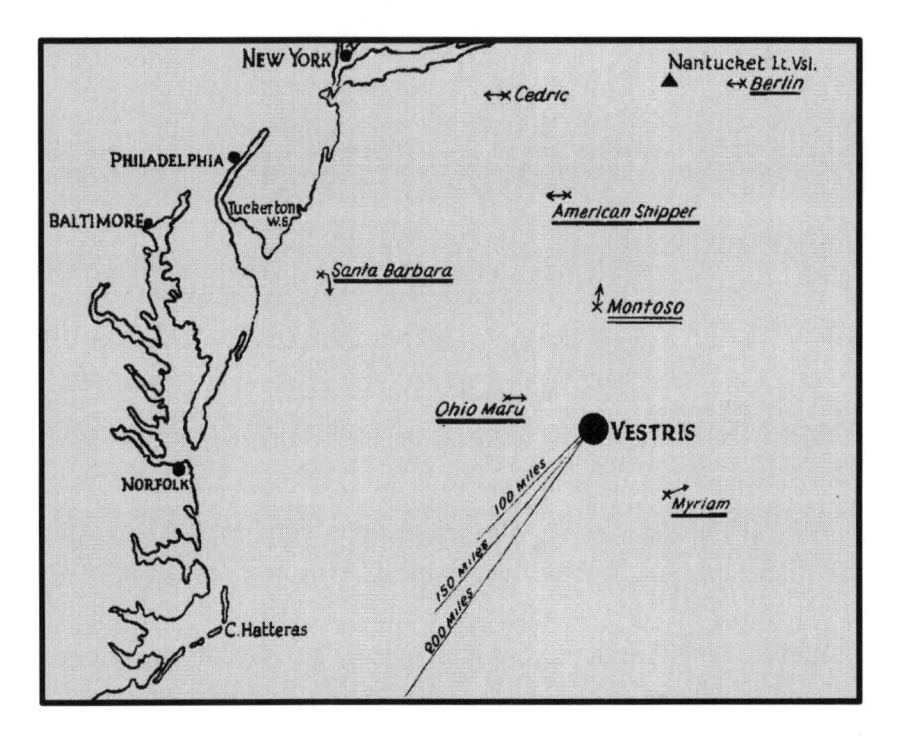

Key rescue vessels and their proximities to the *Vestris*. Adapted from an original diagram by the British Marconi Company. (*Author's collection*.)

Just before 10:00 a.m., Carey ordered Bolger back to the wireless room. "You'd better send the SOS," the first officer told O'Loughlin. "She's thirty-two degrees and going over all the time." Bolger handed O'Loughlin a slip of paper with the ship's position written on it and the

"STAY WITH ME, I'M GOING TO LIVE"

Irishman calmly began tapping out the distress call: "SOS SOS SOS DE CPRV Lat. 37.35 North, Long. 71.08 West. We are heeling over 32 degrees on our starboard side and need immediate assistance"[6] From the smoking room, Paul Dana could hear the antenna snapping out the signal high above. At long last, the rest of the world had a chance to help the *Vestris* and the souls aboard her.

The order to send CQ had come as a surprise to MacDonald, but the instruction to send SOS left him completely floored. Within a few minutes, Finzimer had relayed the message on Tuckerton's powerful transmitter, and added: "All vessels in vicinity to advise position immediately." He then sent word of the *Vestris's* plight to Lamport and Holt's offices in New York City—standard operating procedure when a distress call was received. When the news was learned, company officials had to have lamented the fact their flagship couldn't be sent to her running-mate's aid. The *Voltaire* was still more than 450 miles from the *Vestris*, delayed by the weather and mechanical problems. There was no chance she could make it in time.

Fifty-eight ships received the SOS, but the Grace liner *Santa Barbara* was first to respond: "We will be alongside you *Vestris* at 7:30 p.m." Not all ships were as quick to reply and some never would. The tramp steamer *Montoso* was about twenty-five miles from the *Vestris's* position, en route from Puerto Rico to Boston with a cargo of sugar. Unfortunately, she continued on her course ignorant of the Lamport and Holt liner's struggle. The *Montoso* carried no wireless set. Had her officers been able to hear the SOS, they could have been alongside the *Vestris* within a few hours. The *Montoso's* heartbroken crew members would learn of their proximity to the stricken ship days later when they reached their destination.

---

[6] The wireless code DE signified the word "from." The *Vestris's* call letters were CPRV. Accordingly, the message "DE CPRV" meant "from *Vestris*."

CHAPTER EIGHT

"Do the Best You Can"

Even under the most ideal conditions, the lot of a fireman was an unending amount of backbreaking work in an unspeakably miserable environment. On this day, the severity of the *Vestris's* list was making it nearly impossible for the mostly Barbadian stokers to do their jobs at all.

Quick-thinking Fireman Samuel Parfitt tied a lifeline through the stokehold to help his comrades get around more easily. Others roped themselves together in an effort to prop one another up to stoke the furnaces. It took four men to do the work of one under normal circumstances: one stoker to hold the firebox door open and two to hold up the man who shoveled the coal. It was a good idea, but in practice it didn't really work. Each time the ship lurched in the choppy seas, the ensuing rush of seawater knocked them all down.

The men also had to contend with what amounted to psychological torture. Half-naked stokers held their breath each time the *Vestris* took a deep roll, wondering if it would be the one that finished the ship off. It was enough to turn even the steadiest fireman into a nervous wreck. Still, Adams believed if the men could maintain steam, the pumps would keep the ship afloat until rescue vessels arrived. Unfortunately, conditions were becoming unbearable and the prospect of dying an excruciating death when the ship turned turtle became too much for the men. They began to lose heart.

At about the same time O'Loughlin was tapping out the first SOS, groups of four or so firemen at a time began to quit their posts. Engineers watched incredulously as the men dropped their shovels and took to the ladders in an attempt to make it to the boat deck while there was still time to do so. Although only a handful remained on the job, Adams stayed calm. He sent Sixth Engineer Dickson to the bridge to notify the captain while he followed the stokers up the ladder. The chief thought about stopping off at his cabin to grab his pistol, but in the end he didn't bother. Adams didn't have any ammunition.

Once on deck, the stokers didn't make a dramatic dash for the lifeboats. They simply stretched out on a hatch at the base of the funnel. The firemen weren't there long before Adams arrived and began trying to convince them to go back to work. The chief explained how their presence in the stokehold would keep the ship going. He tried appealing to their sense of duty. Finally he threatened them, but it was no use. They were done. Dickson soon appeared with Carey and Johnson. Someone barked out, "All hands down below!" To which a defiant stoker replied, "We're not going to work anymore." Tensions were running high.

The grandfatherly Carey tried next. "For God's sake go down below, boys, and lend a hand," he pleaded. The captain's presence seemed to do the trick and the stokers began to leave the deck. Dickson went with them. Johnson called out, "Will they be all right with you down below?" The sixth engineer nodded, but it wasn't to be. Upon their return to the stokehold, most of the men immediately went up again by another route.

For Adams and company, trying to force the stokers back to work would be a waste of precious time and energy they didn't have. The engineers resigned themselves to the fact they would have to fire the boilers themselves until the ship went down. Adams, Dickson and the others grabbed shovels and began to feed the fireboxes that ran the pumps and the dynamos that ultimately powered the wireless. Sadly, there weren't enough of them to make much of a difference. With only the engineers and firemen Joseph Boxill, Thomas Ford and Samuel Parfitt stoking, steam pressure began to fall off dramatically.

While the officers were dealing with the stokers, Baptist missionaries E.A. Jackson, his wife Jannette and son Cary sat quietly at a smoking room table. Jannette asked her son to go below to retrieve some personal items, and despite the deck's treacherous slope, Cary was back in a flash with her handbag. As the Jacksons surveyed the scene, they saw passengers arriving in the smoking room without life belts. The family was committed to serving others whether they were in the jungle or aboard a sinking ship. E.A. and Cary dashed below to grab as many life belts as they could carry to give to people who came up without them and had no intention of going below again.

The *Vestris's* life belts were stowed in racks above each bunk. The ship carried nearly 700 for adults and nearly seventy smaller ones for children. With 325 souls aboard, just thirteen of whom were kids or infants, there were more than enough for each person to have two. They were, even by 1928 standards, obsolete—made of cork blocks sewn into a canvas vest. Before long, the Jacksons were back in the smoking room with their arms full of them. They handed the life belts out and helped people put them on correctly.

When they were done, father and son returned to their corner table to find Jannette Jackson with an uneasy look on her face. Grateful men and women followed them over and a small crowd began to huddle near the table. The Reverend stiffened and addressed the group in a low voice, "We must now pray and trust in God to help us." Cary, Jannette and some others bowed their heads. As they prayed, the group was joined by the Headley and Alleyne families. High above, the wireless equipment snapped out the second SOS: "SOS DE CPRV urgent help needed, already 32 degree list to starboard and want help immediately."

At the Tuckerton wireless station, Finzimer sent out a message asking all ships in the vicinity of the *Vestris* to report their positions.

"DO THE BEST YOU CAN"

The Japanese freighter *Ohio Maru* was only fifty miles away. Her skipper replied: "On way now to your assistance." The Marconi men also heard from the *Vestris's* owners: "Wire us immediately your trouble. Lamport." Verchere ran the message to Captain Carey.

The *Vestris's* wireless room. (*Underwood & Underwood*)

While O'Loughlin waited for Verchere to return, he made a duplicate and tossed it into a wire rack. Radio traffic was beginning to pick up, so O'Loughlin and MacDonald decided to work the set alternately, each stepping in for the other while he was on the phone with the bridge or writing down a message. Within fifteen minutes Verchere was back with Carey's response to his employers: "Hove to since yesterday noon, during night developed 32 degree list to starboard, impossible proceed anywhere. Sea moderately rough." In reality, the seas were still a lot worse than moderately rough. O'Loughlin didn't think Carey's message conveyed the gravity of the situation, so he added his own, more specific assessment: "We are getting worse; decks all under water, and ship lying on beam ends." Moments later, Lamport and Holt replied via the Brooklyn Navy Yard:

LAST DANCE OF THE VESTRIS

"Master *Vestris*, U.S.S. *Davis*, destroyer, proceeding to your assistance." The navy operator asked for more information and O'Loughlin quickly obliged: "SOS SOS SOS come at once now, we need immediate assistance, may have to take to the boats any minute now." The *Davis* was 140 miles away and making twenty-eight knots to the stricken ship. The exchange marked the last time the *Vestris* and her owners would ever communicate.

Michael O'Loughlin. (*British National Archives/Craig Stringer*)

Not far from the drama playing out in the wireless room, Cline Slaughter stepped out of his cabin and teetered a few feet before a member of the crew appeared in the hallway. The man answered Slaughter's question about the list by telling him the cargo had shifted slightly and they were in "no danger whatsoever." Satisfied with the explanation, Slaughter went back to his cabin and looked out the porthole. To him, the weather had improved so much compared to the night before he decided to go back to bed. Slaughter undressed and climbed into his bunk.

At 11:00 a.m., a sopping wet, grimy, yet still optimistic Chief Engineer Adams went looking for Carey. He found him halfway down the boat deck looking over the side. "Captain, the water is not gaining anymore," he said. "I am holding it."

"Will you be able to manage it?"

"DO THE BEST YOU CAN"

"I think I can keep her afloat as long as I can keep up steam." Carey told Adams two destroyers would be on scene by 5:00 p.m. and ended the conversation with a plea, "Do the best you can."

As the chief engineer staggered off, a key ship was joining the flotilla of vessels on their way to the *Vestris's* side. After an uneventful crossing from London, passengers aboard the American Merchant Lines' 15,000 ton *S.S. American Shipper* were looking forward to a late Sunday night arrival in New York Harbor. It was not to be. At a few minutes past the hour, Wireless Operator Arthur Jensen heard the *Vestris's* pleas for help. He promptly notified his skipper, 37-year-old Schuyler Cumings. Upon hearing the news, Cumings ordered his ship's course changed and sent word to the *Vestris*: "I am 120 miles North; Proceeding full speed." As the *Shipper* made fifteen knots to the scene of the disaster, Cumings assessed the situation. There were faster vessels much closer to the *Vestris's* position, so he concluded the *Shipper* probably wouldn't make it in time to pick up lifeboats. Instead, the captain believed his mission would most likely be one of support.

Cumings readied his ship to provide medical care to injured survivors and also for the possibility of transporting some of them back to New York. Boat lines were strung along the sides of the ship, pilot ladders were lowered into position and flood lights rigged up. The captain also ordered that cargo nets be prepared in the event anyone had to be hoisted on deck. Cumings then sent for ship's surgeon John Bowlen and warned him to be ready to treat a wide variety of injuries. As word of the rescue mission spread throughout the ship, two women with nursing experience stepped forward to offer Dr. Bowlen additional help if and when anyone was brought on board.

The one-class *American Shipper* could accommodate seventy-five passengers paying the lowest fares on the Atlantic. However, for this voyage only thirty-seven were on board to take advantage of the cheap tickets. Purser Joseph Burrows wasn't sure how many survivors his ship would encounter at the disaster scene, nor did he know where to put them should any be brought aboard. *Shipper* passengers solved the problem for him. Without hesitation, they volunteered their cabins and doubled up in an effort to free up as much space as possible. Officers and crew did the same. Trunks that had been neatly packed for arrival were opened up as passengers prepared to offer their clothing to soaked and miserable survivors. Cooks prepared hot coffee and soup, while stewards stacked blankets on deck. The problem of having enough food for everyone was inadvertently addressed by Burrows days before. He routinely ordered extra in the event the ship was ever held up by bad weather.

In the *American Shipper's* wireless room, Jensen tried using the radio direction finder to determine the exact position of the *Vestris*. Ideally the apparatus could pinpoint the location of any transmission source, but by now the signals coming from the *Vestris* were too weak. Officers would have to rely on coordinates transmitted by the stricken ship and the various shore stations. As the *Shipper* raced through heavy seas, Cumings could only hope they were accurate.

Back on the *Vestris*, E.A. and Cary Jackson weren't the only ones risking their lives for their fellow passengers. A handful of women approached Fred Sorensen to ask if he would go below to fetch their life belts. They looked nervous and afraid, so Sorensen didn't turn them down. He dashed down a flight of stairs and was going cabin-to-cabin looking for extras when he was confronted by a man he recognized as the ship's bartender. Thomas Jones believed Sorensen's errand could cause passengers to panic unnecessarily. "What are you trying to do, frighten them?" Jones asked. "They'll feel better with them on," Sorensen pleaded. The mariner tried to explain, but his argument fell on deaf ears. Jones ordered him not to take anymore life belts out of staterooms, so Sorensen ran to his own cabin and grabbed four from there. When Sorensen's arms were so full he couldn't carry anymore, he ran back up on deck and handed them out. As the women put them on, their eyes welled up with tears.

Others approached Sorensen about getting their life belts, as well. He made several more trips—even to retrieve personal items for people who either couldn't negotiate the sloping decks or who just preferred to remain where they were. Many of the women he helped were wearing only nightgowns and had bare feet. Sorensen went below for their overcoats and shoes. One woman told him where she had

"DO THE BEST YOU CAN"

hidden money in her cabin. Sorensen retrieved it for her. On one of his journeys, Sorensen overheard a crew member telling a passenger the ship was still moving. He shook his head in exasperation. Sorensen knew the *Vestris* had stopped making forward progress the day before.

Despite his heroics, there is a chance Sorensen didn't get every cabin number right. First Class passenger Wallace Sinclair went back to his room to find his new bathrobe missing from the hook where he left it. Sorensen probably snagged it by mistake on one of his trips below.

James and Margaret McCulloch worked side-by-side in the ship's laundry room. Before the events of the past twenty-four hours, the only unwanted water they had to contend with came from their leaky washing machine and the rotten porthole in their quarters. McCulloch went on deck to get a better understanding of the state of affairs. He had been at sea for just under three decades and had experienced just about everything the ocean could dish out. After a quick look around, McCulloch's greatest fear was confirmed. He went below to get his wife. It took him several precious minutes to work his way back through the leaning halls and stairways. "She's about to turn over," he told Margaret when he found her. "Get some clothes and let's go."

Seasick Mormon missionaries Huish and Burt were still hunkered down in their cabin when they heard loud voices in the hallway outside. Huish went to investigate and saw a steward helping a woman to the boat deck. When she noticed the missionary peering through the crack of his cabin door, she gasped. "For heaven's sake, boy, get out of your room," she yelled. "This ship is going to sink!" By this time, Burt had joined his companion at the door. As the pair shuffled past, Huish asked if he needed his life belt. "Oh I guess you'd better take one along for safety," the steward said. "But I don't think you'll need it." The two disappeared down the forward end of the hallway. The missionaries grabbed their life belts and prepared to leave their cabin for good. "We'd better take our money and passports," Burt said.

"We might not need them anymore," Huish countered.

"Oh yes, we will."

The now completely fed up Fred Puppe wrongly assumed Carey hadn't sent out an SOS, but he was in the smoking room, and the place was a clearing house for rumors—some of them conjured up purposely to fool people. Purely to cheer the women, Edward Walcott and some others made up the story another ship was close by and rushing to their aid. It seemed to work, although Walcott himself wondered if the *Vestris* could hold out long enough for the vessel to arrive even if it were true. Puppe looked anxiously around the room at his fellow passengers and hoped the crew would begin loading the lifeboats. In case they did, Puppe helped his wife and baby outside and began scanning the sea for the vessels he prayed would arrive soon.

Paul Dana noticed the children on the boat deck were well-bundled, as their mothers assumed they would eventually have to leave the ship. To his right, a woman wept softly. In her arms was a frightened little boy. Mother and son were looking over the port side rail at the rolling sea when Dana tried cheering the boy up. "Isn't this fun?" he asked with a smile. The child looked up at his mother and nodded sadly. She reached up to wipe tears from her eyes.

Jorge do Valle was also ready to go, but he was missing one small detail—his shoes. The Third Class passenger figured he would be able to swim better without them. Further down the deck, Carey was asking Second Steward Duncan where the passengers were and whether they were wearing their life belts. Duncan told him most were ready and waiting in the smoking room. The second steward knew the ship couldn't hold out much longer, but he also realized the passengers were famished. He was determined to do his job. Duncan went to the smoking room, gathered up as many sore-shouldered stewards as he could find and asked for volunteers to help him fetch food for the passengers. There was silence, and then an outright refusal. "I wouldn't go down there for a thousand dollars," one man said. Duncan had to go alone.

There were five clinker-built lifeboats under davits on each side of the ship, with four additional boats strapped to the poop deck.[7] Altogether there were enough seats to accommodate eight hundred

---

[7] Clinker-built boats are made of overlapping wood planks, like a clapboard house.

passengers and crew. The math was easy to do. Every one of the 327 souls on board was guaranteed a seat. Loading and launching the boats correctly would be the keys to survival.

First Class smoking room. (*Author's collection*)

The *Vestris* was now listing thirty-five degrees to port. Consequently, the lifeboats on that side of the ship were much farther away from the water than their starboard counterparts. Carey was left with a momentous decision—selecting the safest side from which to load and launch them. He watched as the wind buffeted passengers lining the port side rails. The powerful gusts only added to their misery, as they could barely stand to begin with. Carey became convinced there was no way anyone could make it to the starboard side. The captain decided to load the port side boats, but it would prove to be a bad call. The *Vestris* was actually functioning as a wall of sorts, sheltering the starboard side boats from the wind and waves. Passengers would have had a much easier time climbing into them and Carey should have found a way to get people down there.

At 11:30 a.m., the captain finally gave in and issued the order he'd been putting off all morning. "Take to the boats," he commanded.

"Women and children first." The latter would prove to be a major mistake. The decision to give select passengers preference was a vestige from a bygone era and the captain should have known better. With enough space for everyone, passengers and crew should have been evenly distributed in all boats. Carey's decision to ignore boat assignments would break up families needlessly.

The captain elected to direct the loading of the port side's even-numbered boats with help from Bolger and Watson. Chief Officer Johnson was assigned the odd-numbered starboard boats, while Welland was given the job of launching the four on the poop deck. Johnson made his way to the starboard side with great difficulty. As he staggered along the deck, he found himself grabbing onto hapless passengers in an effort to keep his balance.

Years earlier, *Shipbuilder* magazine published a fully illustrated article describing one of the most important pieces of lifesaving equipment on the *Vestris*. The ship was the first in the world to be equipped with state-of-the-art hand-cranked Martin davits, which the reporter noted were "severely tested" by the Board of Trade before being approved for use. The piece went on to describe their user-friendliness:

> On board the *Vestris* the operation of running out and launching a boat has been accomplished by one man in less than a minute and a half, the actual time occupied in one of the tests being one minute and twenty seconds to bring the boat outboard, and seven minutes to lower it from the davits to the water.

In practice, the operation would be completely different. For an unknown reason, crewmen were ordered to ignore lifeboat No. 2, the forward most boat on the port side, and instead prepare the next three boats aft for loading. Sailors fumbled as they uncovered No. 4 and hoisted it clumsily out of its chocks. Fred Puppe watched them with disgust. It looked to him like the men were doing it for the first time in their lives, and some of them probably were. During drills, the lifeboats were merely uncovered and swung out. Sailors weren't required to

"DO THE BEST YOU CAN"

lower them all the way to the water or test the releasing gear but once per voyage—a single occasion every two months. Now they had to get it right, under extreme pressure and with frightened and judgmental passengers like Puppe glaring at them.

Second Steward Duncan reappeared from below and began handing out the Fig Newtons he'd found. All the while, he kept up a cheerful countenance. "It's absolutely safe," Duncan said as he went about. "In two hours you won't know that anything has ever been wrong with the ship." Dr. Lehner watched him work. He thought Duncan looked as happy as if he'd just been married. Besides the second steward's cheery pronouncements, it was quiet except for the wind, the waves and the ship's death groans.

Just as Keith Burt and David Huish hobbled into the smoking room, Huish slipped, tumbled into a chair and smashed it to bits. Once outside, the missionaries had to lean against the bulkhead or hang onto the railing to keep from falling down. Burt and Huish were watching the crew prepare the lifeboats when Huish asked a crewman if the ship was in any danger. "No," he said. "The ship could go on like this for a week, probably." Huish thought it was complete fantasy, so he asked why, if the ship was safe, they were being lowered at all. "Just a matter of precaution," the man told him. Huish and Burt tied their life belts on over their coats.

No steward knocked on Cline and Wilma Slaughter's cabin door to warn them of danger, nor did one have to. Inside, the coat on the hook was serving as an alarm for the young couple as it stuck out at an ever-worsening angle. Slaughter pulled himself out of bed once more in an attempt to try and figure out what was going on once and for all. This time he took his wife with him. When the two stepped out of their cabin, they ran into their steward almost immediately. Cline and Wilma became the recipients of an unusual piece of information that morning—the truth. The steward told them no matter what the officers said, the *Vestris* would sink—and soon. He advised them to put their life belts on and get up to the boats. The Slaughters returned to their cabin. Cline helped Wilma put on her life belt and shuffled her out the door for the last time.

LAST DANCE OF THE VESTRIS

Starboard lifeboats hang in their davits. *(P&A)*

In the engine room, seawater was pouring in on engineers' heads from the coal bunkers above and, because the bilges were full, was lapping over the floor plates on which they stood. When Adams returned from his conference with Carey, there was trouble almost immediately in the form of a massive leak in the bulkhead above the gauges. An enormous quantity of water was spurting through the seams. Suddenly, the steel could take no more and the tremendous pressure tore the bulkhead open with a great crash, sending thousands of gallons of water black with coal dust cascading into the engine room. Moments later, pressure in the coal bunker above the starboard boiler caused it to rupture, as well. Adams waded to the telephone to alert the bridge. The chief engineer told the voice on the other end to tell the captain what happened. Adams knew nothing more could be done to save the *Vestris*, but in the tradition of the *Titanic* engineers, he and his men decided to remain at their posts in an effort to keep the dynamos going as long as possible.

CHAPTER NINE

"Do they Really Mean It?"

No siren ever sounded to alert passengers to prepare to abandon ship. Instead, word passed from person to person. Sorensen thought it spread like a rumor. He stood next to adventurous widow Mabel Mills on the boat deck and noticed she was shivering, but on the relatively warm day it wasn't because she was cold. When Mills learned she would have to leave the ship, she turned to Sorensen and asked, "Do they really mean it?"

"Certainly they mean it," he answered. Mills, who was traveling First Class on holiday, would be dead in a few hours' time.

Although they were under intense pressure, officers remained cheerful and relaxed, but of little assistance to confused passengers who didn't know their boat stations. In addition, Johnson never finished the crew's boat assignments. The end result was scores of people milling about the tilted deck with no idea where to go.

Making matters worse, sailors had made little progress preparing the port side lifeboats. The boats were still resting on the steel plates of the ship's hull, too far from the sea to load safely. Somehow, the crew would have to get them much closer to the water. Sailors tried solving the problem by using oars to pry the heavy boats up and inch them down the side of the ship, but it didn't work. With each heave, the rivet heads on the steel plates carved deep grooves into the wooden boats—in some cases splitting the clapboard apart. Finally the crew devised a way to slide them down the bumpy hull. Oars and planks—even stretchers were jammed underneath to serve as rails. It worked, but progress was still painfully slow and anxious passengers were beginning to reach their wits' end as they watched. Herbert Johnston was one who believed there was a better option. He approached a crew member. "For God's sake lower some of the starboard boats," he pleaded. "Oh no," the man said. "We can get those down anytime and we're lowering these first because they're the most difficult."

"Well if you don't watch out they'll all go down with the ship," Johnston cautioned.

When No. 4, No. 6 and No. 8 had each been worked painstakingly to within about fifteen feet of the water, Jacob's ladders were tied to the railing and laid on the ship's side. Terrified women began to line up to make the treacherous climb over the rail and down the hull to the boats. Once they were safely seated, sailors passed their children down in slings made of blankets.

Joseph Wilson, his wife Mary and their two sons were returning home to Brazil where Joseph worked for a telephone company. As they waited to climb into a boat, Mary was trying to console 3-year-old Francis and 1-year-old Paul by kissing and cuddling them as they squirmed. Sorensen was watching her try to keep a grip on the boys when a Barbadian woman appeared and caused a stir on the relatively quiet boat deck. She was belting out a hymn about "going down in the water," despite a man's best attempts to stop her. The crazed singing rattled passengers and crew—including the normally cool Sorensen, but he took pity on the woman, figuring she had probably lost her mind. He didn't know her name, but it may have been 50-year-old deportee Sarah Leacock, who was being sent back to Barbados for being "insane." When it was finally her turn to climb into one of the boats, the woman froze on the ladder and it took sailors several

"DO THEY REALLY MEAN IT?"

minutes to get her moving again. Sorensen eventually helped Mary Wilson negotiate the ship's hull into lifeboat No. 6. When she was settled, he handed her boys to her. William Wills Davies occupied the cabin across the hall from the Wilsons. He remembered seeing the boys several times the night before, with baby Paul giggling and cooing as he sat in his stroller. Now, Davies was shocked at the image of the boys waiting to leave the ship in the middle of the Atlantic.

Herbert Johnston was on to something when he suggested loading the starboard boats. With the superstructure in the way, most of his fellow passengers couldn't see what was happening on the other side of the ship. Consequently, they were unable to assess their chances with the boats there. Second Officer Watson thought loading them was worth a try, so he and Duncan found three willing ladies on the port side and began the trek across. The group made their way down the deck with great difficulty, taking full advantage of lifelines sailors had strung across the ship. When they were safely on the starboard side, Watson saw a lifeboat in the water close by. It was still hanging from its davits with only a handful of crewmen aboard. This is the boat they would try for. To make it, the women would have to jump into the water and paddle close enough to be hauled in. It was a distance of only a few feet, but it looked too dangerous and they refused. Watson and Duncan tried coaxing them, but it was no use. The ladies finally demanded that they be taken back up.

The sloping deck above must have looked like Mount Everest to Watson, but he did as he was asked and the group began to climb. Watson and Duncan struggled along the lifeline for a full twenty minutes, pushing and pulling the passengers up inch by painful inch. When they finally reached the port side, the women melted back into the crowd. Unfazed, Watson asked some others to try, but nobody took advantage of the opportunity. The second officer gave up.

Meanwhile, Laundry Stewards James and Margaret McCulloch decided to try their luck with No. 4 boat. James helped Margaret down the hull. Next to board was Second Class passenger Helen Cubbin. In one arm, she held a baby boy; with her free hand she clutched the arm of a little girl. The children screamed in terror at the commotion around them.

Lack of sleep coupled with a tremendous amount of psychological pressure had taken its toll on Captain Carey. He was unshaven and looked haggard in a rumpled blue overcoat. To some he appeared angry, to others bewildered. Carey wore no hat or collar, but perhaps most disturbingly, he also neglected to put on a life belt. In any case, the captain's fatigue showed and passengers were becoming concerned for his well-being. "Women and children to the right," he barked as he made his way toward Watson. The second officer asked if it was time to launch the lifeboats. "Go ahead, you might as well let them down," Carey said. "Only lower one boat at a time or you'll have one on top of the other."

Further down the boat deck, Carlos Quiros and William Wills Davies were startled by what sounded like a gunshot. Well aware of the state Carey was in, Quiros turned to Davies, "The captain has shot himself!" The men looked around and saw Carey alive and well, directing the crew. A relieved Quiros figured the sound had been an explosion of steam from somewhere below, leading him to believe the end was growing closer. He told Davies, "Time to go."

In the wireless room, O'Loughlin was apologizing for what he believed was sloppy sending: "It's the devil to work with this list. Lifeboats are now out." Radio waves across the Eastern Seaboard came alive as the *Vestris's* situation became known to more and more ships. At about noon, the *S.S. Berlin* of the North German Lloyd radioed: "Will reach you at 10 p.m." The liner was bound for New York and was two hundred miles away. She immediately turned south and headed for the *Vestris's* position at full speed. O'Loughlin replied with more information: "Am lying on starboard beam ends, decks awash." MacDonald ran to tell the captain the good news. He found Carey working on lifeboat No. 6. MacDonald grabbed him by the sleeves to get his attention. "As regards being picked up, you can rest easy on that point," the Marconi man said. "There is a German ship, the *Berlin*, fitted with a direction finder, and she is coming down."

"Are you OK in the wireless room?" Carey asked.

"DO THEY REALLY MEAN IT?"

"Yes, sir, just leave it to us." MacDonald went back to the office. At a quarter past noon O'Loughlin sent Tuckerton an update: "It is bad enough in this situation, old man, let alone position the ship is in, can hardly stay and receive."

"OK," Finzimer replied. Despite the worsening situation, O'Loughlin was tenacious: "SOS SOS SOS we will soon have to abandon now."

Most of the starboard boats had been launched by the time Fred Hanson took this photo. The Martin davits are in the foreground. (*Wide World*)

Wave after wave drilled the *Vestris*. After each, the ship shuddered frighteningly. Passengers and crew wondered if the next jolt would signal the end. It was after one such impact the *Vestris* lurched suddenly, causing No. 8 boat to swing out and crash back against the ship's side. The violence of the collision opened a six-inch gash just above the lifeboat's waterline. An outraged William Wills Davies pointed it out to a crewman. "Once this boat gets into the water it will swell up and become watertight," the man told him. Davies found the explanation to be completely absurd.

LAST DANCE OF THE VESTRIS

Despite their belief the boat wasn't seriously damaged, some members of the crew *would* try to patch the hole. Within minutes, a pair of sailors appeared on deck with hammers, a strip of tin and a few nails. As incredulous passengers watched, the men placed the metal over the gash and pounded four nails into it, one in each corner. The pessimistic Davies was sure the boat would still sink if it ever reached the water. It wasn't long before Carey shuffled up to check on No. 8's progress. Anne Devore, who was seated in the boat with her husband Earl and the Battens, called his attention to the feeble attempt at a repair. "Captain isn't it dangerous to send people out in a boat of this shape?" she asked. The ashen-faced Carey turned away without answering.

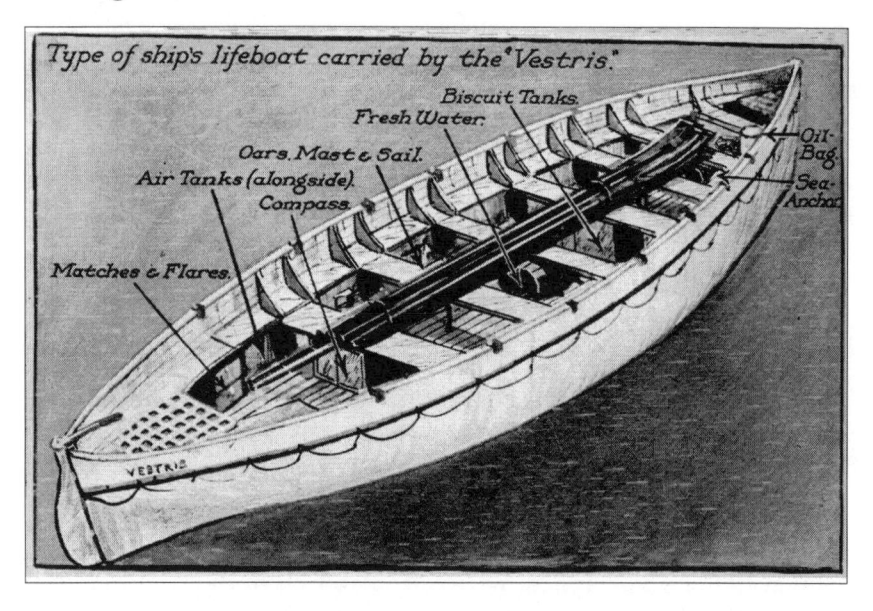

Equipment carried by a typical lifeboat. From a drawing by G.H. Davis in *The Illustrated London News*. (*Author's collection*)

Fred Puppe took his family aft to search for a boat, but a crewman sent them forward again. It wasn't long before sailors were helping Charlotte and the baby into lifeboat No. 4. Puppe was climbing down the rope ladder after them when a booming voice called him back. "Don't let that man on," Carey commanded the sailor next to him.

"DO THEY REALLY MEAN IT?"

"Don't let another man aboard." Puppe looked up at Carey, then down at his family and wondered why he was being singled out. "But my wife and child are there and other husbands, too," he pleaded. The sailor stepped in to mediate. "Your wife and child are safe," he said. "Don't overcrowd the boat. Go to another. They will be saved long before you are." Despite his growing rage, Puppe did as he was told. He waved a quick good-bye to Charlotte and climbed back aboard the ship.

As O'Loughlin and MacDonald began testing the battery-powered emergency wireless set, an electrician stopped by to warn them Adams was about to shut down the boilers. It meant the end for the dynamo that generated the ship's electricity. O'Loughlin told him he was already anticipating the loss of power and turned back to his work. His sending began to reflect the worsening situation, but he was still crystal clear: "Our steam is gone, power getting low, will use emergency set, please listen for same." Tuckerton to *Vestris*: "*OK.*" And then a few minutes later: "SOS SOS Power cut off. Am going to use emergency set."

It wasn't long before the set's batteries started to die. It was also looking increasingly likely they would detach from the wall and crash down on the men. Nevertheless, even as the signals faded, more ships were advising they were on their way. Welcome news came from the battleship *U.S.S. Wyoming*: "Will reach you at 9 p.m." Sadly, O'Loughlin knew the *Vestris* wouldn't be around when the dreadnought arrived. He replied: "Can't wait any longer, going to abandon."

O'Loughlin sent Verchere to track down life belts and within a few minutes the teenager returned with three. Verchere and MacDonald put theirs on right away, but O'Loughlin elected to sit on his for better balance. While on his errand, Verchere noticed some of the lifeboats had gone and he explained that if they didn't leave the wireless room right away, there wouldn't be any left to get into. O'Loughlin, focused on his work, ignored him. Tuckerton couldn't hear the *Vestris* anymore, but some ships and shore stations could still make out a faint whisper: "We are abandoning ship. We are taking to the lifeboats."

Now it was MacDonald's turn to make the case to try for a boat. "Well c'mon you two, there's nothing more we can do," he pleaded.

71

Reluctantly, O'Loughlin gave it up. He tapped out a final message from the *Vestris*: "So long, Tuckerton, SK."[8] MacDonald dropped out the hole in the floor that used to be the port side doorway, while Verchere and O'Loughlin climbed out the starboard door—now a rectangle in the ceiling. "Sparks" left without his lifebelt.

The quiet and reserved O'Loughlin was a consummate professional to the end. Wireless operators along the Eastern Seaboard would later marvel at his coolness under pressure, observing that his work was so steady and devoid of mistakes, it seemed impossible it was originating from a horribly listing, sinking ocean liner.

Meanwhile, things had become so bad in the engine room the starboard side was completely under water and it was knee high and rising on the port side. A despondent Chief Engineer Adams began shutting down the boilers and pumps. The water started to gain immediately. In an effort to prevent explosions when the ship succumbed, Adams asked for volunteers for the treacherous assignment of shutting down the main steam valves. Fourth Engineer George Prestwich and Fifth Engineer John Jones climbed atop the boilers to do the job. Jones had been in bed on doctor's orders, but the 25-year-old returned to work earlier that morning to help out.

No one ever came down to tell the engineers to abandon ship. When Adams, Prestwich and Jones climbed the ladders to try for the deck, they became last men out of the *Vestris's* engine room. The chief engineer went to his cabin to get his life belt. He and Prestwich would eventually make it into a boat. Jones would die a hero.

---

[8] SK was the wireless code for "all transmission is complete."

CHAPTER TEN

"My God, My God, I am Not to Blame for This"

There was nothing left on the bridge for Quartermaster Lionel Licorish to do. The ship wasn't going anywhere, so the 23-year-old Barbadian figured he'd be of more use helping with the lifeboats. Licorish tied the wheel down in its "hard-over" position and joined Carey and Watson on the boat deck.

The captain and his second officer were well aware the *Vestris* would sink, but they still held to the belief the ship could remain afloat for hours more. Fireman Samuel Parfitt watched as two men approached Carey for direction. "What about the crew, what shall we do with them?" they asked. Parfitt heard Carey tell them, "Damn the crew." He became so angry he took off running for the poop deck lifeboats. Parfitt and another fireman tried to push No. 12 into a position where it could be lowered, but it was no use. Despite their best efforts to free it, the boat wouldn't budge. "There's time enough for me to look for heaven," Parfitt thought. "Now is the time to look for life." The pair slid down to No. 11, where they were joined by three other crewmen. Compared to No. 12, the boat was relatively easy to launch. They decided to row as far away from the *Vestris* as they could to avoid the suction they were sure would come when she sank, then return to pick up swimmers.

Fifty mile per hour wind gusts blasted the passengers sitting in the boats on the ship's port side, as well as those still waiting to climb into them. Dr. Lehner tried to get into No. 8, but like Puppe, was ordered out by Carey. Pretty newlywed Gladys Stevens descended the same rope ladder, but when her husband saw the tin patch, he made her get out. Instead, Orrin Stevens helped her into No. 6, where he believed she would be safer. The boat was filling up quickly. Sailors passed babies and small children to waiting Pantryman Jean Gladianes, who handed them to their mothers. When the boat was nearly full, Storekeeper George Amsdell hopped in and the order was given to lower it the remaining distance to the sea. Orrin Stevens coolly bade his wife farewell and linked up with Fred Puppe to look for a boat. The scene repeated itself over and over. First Class passenger Edward Johnson watched husbands and wives say good-bye to one another "without display of emotion."

Purser Albert Pugh spent most of his time with the passengers in the smoking room, doing what he could to make them comfortable. He was convinced everyone was topside, but he decided to go below one last time to make sure. Pugh went staggering through the tilted First Class hallways banging on cabin doors. He didn't find anyone, so he decided to attempt a rescue of a different kind. Pugh went to the bridge, grabbed the ship's papers, including the log, stuffed them into a dispatch case and returned to the boat deck. He handed it to a steward who gave it to a sailor in lifeboat No. 6. The papers made it just in time.

Ropes creaked and strained as No. 6 scraped along the ship's side toward the sea. However, when the boat was about five feet from the water, the falls ran out of slack and it jolted to a stop. The lifeboat hung there for several minutes until someone yelled for the rope to be cut. Storekeeper Amsdell grabbed a knife, yelled for everyone to hang on and began to saw through the aft falls. It was a tense few moments.

"MY GOD, MY GOD, I AM NOT TO BLAME FOR THIS"

Everyone knew if one end of the boat was cut free and the other held fast, the women and children would be spilled into the sea. Some of the crewmen jumped out and scampered back aboard the sinking *Vestris*, but as Amsdell cut the last rope the forward falls released simultaneously and No. 6 hit the water cleanly.

Purser Albert Pugh (left) and Chief Engineer James Adams. (*British National Archives/Craig Stringer*)

The greatly relieved passengers were just beginning to row away when the end came for most of them. A heavy steel beam snapped off the *Vestris* with a loud crack. Whether it was a cargo crane or a davit, the beam fell so fast no one really had a chance to see exactly what it was or where it came from. Steward George Hogg was standing on deck, directly in its path. He screamed as the beam shattered his arms on its way down, bouncing off the hull before dropping directly into No. 6 with a sickening thud. Most of the women and children on board were crushed to death instantly. In a split second, the hands of Pantryman Gladianes were shredded and one of his arms was snapped like a twig. The head of the infant he was holding was smashed to a bloody pulp.

Nearly everyone who survived the impact was spilled into the sea; others ended up in the water when the shattered lifeboat sank. Children wailed as they drowned. Joseph Wilson jumped over the *Vestris's* side to rescue his wife and sons. None of the Wilsons were ever seen again.

Hogg staggered back, both of his arms broken and blinded in one eye. The case containing the ship's vital papers was lost.

Storekeeper Amsdell was trying to swim with a broken arm and a head injury when a wave washed him back onto the ship's side. He immediately jumped back into the sea and grabbed onto a floating piece of wreckage. No one saw what became of Gladys Stevens. She and dozens of others were dead or drowning, but their husbands and fathers didn't know it. Like Orrin Stevens, they had gone aft believing their families to be safe and didn't see the "white thing" drop into the boat that was supposed to have been their salvation.

Moments after lifeboat No. 6 was destroyed, Pantryman Fred Hanson again appeared with his camera. Hanson was not a trained photojournalist and the fact was reflected in his work thus far. Hanson's first exposures were evidence he lacked an eye for capturing the humanity of an event. However, in a matter of a few days the scenes he photographed would become known the world over. Hanson was standing on the port side near the bridge looking aft. The deck was littered with the ropes and spars sailors were using to slide the boats down the hull. Steward Hogg leaned against a bulkhead helplessly, his face contorted in pain. Hanson steadied himself and looked through his viewfinder. In the foreground were five or six men pulling on a rope as they worked to launch lifeboat No. 4. One of them, a young man in a white steward's jacket, looked ominously over his shoulder. A handful of men peered over the rail—scanning the waves for anyone who may have survived the wreck of lifeboat No. 6. In the distance, a crowd of passengers jostled to get into No. 10, which still hung in its davits. Hanson pushed the button and the moment was frozen in time.

Years later, the Chicago Tribune explained why the photograph resonated through the decades:

> The steward's face is the tragic mask that completes the picture and gives it classic value. It expresses excitement, fatigue, nervous strain and dynamic resolution. Many a man has looked like that in a desperate crisis on sea or land and when the full story has been told he has been called a hero.

"MY GOD, MY GOD, I AM NOT TO BLAME FOR THIS"

Within the next few minutes, the *Vestris* would begin its two mile descent to the bottom of the ocean. The passengers knew it, yet they still made their way to the boats in an orderly fashion. Members of the crew were also trying to escape the ship. Carey noticed Trimmer Fritz Gittens trying to climb into lifeboat No. 10. "Where are you going?" the captain yelled. "Go away." Gittens slid across to the starboard side in the hopes of having better luck there.

As it turned out, Dr. Lehner caught a lucky break when he was prevented from entering doomed No. 6. Now he climbed down the ladder to get into No. 10. He took a final glance up at the men who were still waiting to board. Lehner recognized one of them as Cary Jackson. He became the last person to see the teen alive. Belvedere College of Dublin graduate William Burke was on the same rope ladder. Like Lehner he looked up, but he instead made eye contact with Captain Carey, who was standing directly above him. Burke called out, "Cheerio captain, Jolly Old Ireland!" Carey smiled sadly back.

By this time, August Groman had mustered the strength to claw his way out of the stairway he had fallen into. He and his friend William Adams reunited and climbed into No. 10. The lifeboat's capacity was sixty-one and it was filling up fast. Fifty-seven people were on board including Burke, Lehner, Fred Puppe and Orrin Stevens. The men yelled for an officer to join them, but none came forward. Carlos Quiros had a foot in the boat when he had second thoughts. "I'm not going to get into something that I'll have to get out of," he whispered to himself. Quiros stepped back onto the ship only to discover he had been separated from Davies. He looked around, but his friend was nowhere to be found. Left with no other option, Quiros jumped over the side. No. 10 was lowered the remaining distance to the sea and was about to cast off when the releasing gear failed. Terrified passengers knew if it couldn't be freed they would go down with the ship.

The releasing gear consisted of a handle near the boat's stern connected by a chain to both the forward and aft hook blocks. A firm tug on the handle should have dropped the boat into the water, but the equipment rarely performed as designed. Most of the badly corroded chains snapped, rendering the entire apparatus useless.

The most iconic of Alfred Hanson's photographs, taken from the port side boat deck of the sinking *Vestris*. (*Corbis*)

"MY GOD, MY GOD, I AM NOT TO BLAME FOR THIS"

Sailors chopped frantically at No. 10's ropes with dull hatchets with no effect. A quick-thinking passenger finally cut them with his pocket knife and the boat dropped into the sea and rowed clear of the ship. When No. 10 was about a football field away from the *Vestris,* Fred Puppe looked back to try and locate the boat his family was in. He saw two port side boats still attached to the ship and knew Charlotte and Lisolette were in one of them. Puppe was furious. He had been promised his loved ones would be saved before he was. Now that he'd left the ship, there was nothing he could do for them but watch and wait.

Fred Hanson stood a few steps from the place where he shot what would become his most famous photograph and pointed his camera aft once more. The scene had changed slightly in the thirty minutes since he took it. Lifeboat No. 10 and the gathering of men waiting to climb into it were gone, but poor Hogg hadn't moved from his position against the bulkhead. What made this new scene so chilling was the man staggering along the deck in Hanson's direction. Whether he was a crewman or a passenger couldn't be determined by looking at his clothes—it was obvious he hastily threw them on as he rushed up on deck. The man's hair was wild and his eyes were clear. When the shutter snapped, he was looking directly at Hanson. The pantryman put his camera away and, as many of his shipmates were doing, headed for the starboard side of the ship.

As time ran out, there was still an absence of panic while passengers looked for space in the remaining lifeboats. Unfortunately, there was an abundance of confusion. Norman and Marion Batten were assigned to lifeboat No. 10, but for reasons unknown to the couple they were ordered into No. 8 instead. The lifeboat was resting on the *Vestris's* hull about six feet from the water, but the Battens managed to climb in safely.

Paul Dana *was* assigned to No 8. It was almost full, but he made his way down the ladder and joined about sixty others, including the Battens, the Devores and their dog Speedway Lady, Major Inouye and his wife Teruko, Second Class passenger Clytie Raphael, Third Class passenger Elvira Rua and Stewardess Clara Ball. Some crewmen

79

including Fireman Gerald Burton hopped in, but since there was no officer to command the boat, Sorensen's old friend, Bartender Thomas Jones was put in charge.

As fortune would have it, Dana saw Sorensen standing at the rail. "Come on, we need you skipper," he yelled. Sorensen had other ideas. He thought the boats were in such bad shape he would stay on the ship until the end and take his chances in the water. He wanted to help, but of all the lifeboats on board, Sorensen considered No. 8 the one he would be sure to avoid. It was a tough call for the seaman, but in the end he changed his mind and climbed in by holding onto a rope and mountaineering down the hull.

When Charles Verchere arrived at his assigned boat, he looked down and wondered how he was going to get in. No. 4 was still stuck on the ship's side, five feet from the water. Between forty and fifty passengers were inside, including women and children. Officers debated what to do. They determined if the boat was released from where it was, it would tip and spill everyone into the sea. Somehow it would have to be lowered even closer to the water. Verchere decided he'd seen enough. He opted to stay out of No. 4 and find another way off the ship. Verchere sat down on the deck and slid to the starboard side, where he ran into Johnson. The chief officer ordered him into lifeboat No. 7. Verchere had to climb over the davits and down the falls, but he made it safely and joined about a dozen other crewmen in the boat. When it was time to launch, the releasing gear failed and the men had to chop the ropes with hatchets to get the boat free.

After seeing No. 7 off, Johnson moved aft to No. 9. The boat was hanging close to the water with only Second Wireless Operator MacDonald and a handful of other crewmen aboard. The forward falls were jammed, but the aft gear looked like it would release cleanly. It would be a gamble. With the ocean rolling beneath the boat, Johnson would have to saw through the rope and time his cut perfectly to free No. 9 without dumping everyone into the sea. "Now when I say pull, you pull," Johnson ordered. MacDonald warned, "Hold onto the sides, she will shake you out!" As Johnson cut through he yelled "Pull," but the aft releasing gear failed as the swell disappeared from beneath the boat and it tipped bow first into the water. Everyone held on for their lives as the sea surged in and washed the oars and supplies away. Sailors were eventually able to release the falls, but not before the boat was full of water. Swamped, No. 9 barely floated free from the ship.

Quartermaster Elton Clarke was helping to launch No. 3, but he became concerned for its safety when he noticed the ship's funnel leaning precariously over the boat. Other crewmen hopped in, but Clarke stayed out, believing the funnel would fall and crush everyone to death the next time the *Vestris* rolled. It did not. When Clarke was satisfied the lifeboat was out of danger, he jumped into the sea and was hauled in. No. 3 rowed away with only eleven of the ship's crew on board. Its capacity was sixty.

Meanwhile, Johnson had moved all the way forward to No. 1 boat. He found only four crewmen aboard including Fred Hanson, who pointed his camera over the side to snap one last photo. Besides himself, the only person left on deck was First Officer Bolger, who had come over from the port side. "Come, get into this boat," Johnson ordered. "I am not going in the boat, I am going to go back again," Bolger shot back. Johnson didn't insist and the first officer ran off to climb up to the port side to help Carey. Bolger should have obeyed his superior. His decision would cost him his life.

With Bolger out of the picture, Johnson put Carpenter Gus Wohld in charge of No. 1 and cleared it for launch. It was the only powered lifeboat on board, but Wohld and company couldn't figure out how to run the motor. Regulations called for it to be crewed by an engineer, but since there wasn't one around, the men would have to row. As the boat was lowered to the sea, Hanson wrapped two rolls of exposures in a piece of oilcloth to prevent them from getting wet and stuffed them into his pocket. No. 1 hit the water, released cleanly and the men began to row away. As they did, Johnson yelled for them to go to the other side of the ship to pick up swimmers.

The starboard Martin davits were all deployed and empty. With all the boats in the water, the chief officer looked around and saw there was nothing left for him to do. Like Bolger, he tried climbing up to the port side to offer assistance to Carey and the others, but the incline of the deck was so bad he couldn't make it across. After trying and failing a number of times, he gave up. Johnson noticed swamped No. 9 boat floating near the side of the ship, so he jumped into the sea and swam to it. With great difficulty, the men rowed around to the *Vestris's* port side where they saw lifeboats No. 4 and No. 8 still hanging from their davits. As the boat was tossed by the waves, a seasick James MacDonald hung his head over the side to vomit.

Chief Officer Frank Johnson (left) and Third Officer Herbert Welland. (*British National Archives/Craig Stringer*)

On lifeboat No. 4, the terrified children Helen Cubbin was minding screamed despite her best attempts to calm them down. Mormon missionaries Burt and Huish climbed in and sat down next to one another. Laundryman James McCulloch helped the last few passengers down the ladders and hopped into the boat. With the ship heeling over, McCulloch held onto his wife. Waiter Isaac Scott had a feeling something was about to go wrong. He began pleading with the others to get out, to no avail. He scrambled back onto the ship alone.

By this time, passengers had figured out that some of the starboard lifeboats had gotten away with only crew on board. The realization came too late to make any difference. Earlier, Herbert Johnston was emphatic about loading them. Now he watched incredulously as a handful of mostly empty starboard boats rowed away from the ship. He decided one of them would be his ticket to survival.

"MY GOD, MY GOD, I AM NOT TO BLAME FOR THIS"

Johnston jumped overboard and swam toward them, finally making it to No. 3. He was hauled in.

Quartermaster Lionel Licorish staggered up to No. 12 boat on the poop deck and like Samuel Parfitt did, found it firmly attached to the deck. He didn't waste time trying to free it because No. 14 was lying unfastened nearby. There was no way to launch the boat properly so Licorish worked to make sure it would float free when the ship sank. When he was done, Licorish jumped over the port side railing, slid down the hull and plopped into the sea. He swam a long distance off to avoid suction and waited for the *Vestris* to go under. Licorish didn't have to tread water very long.

As the *Vestris* began her death roll, Second Steward Duncan approached Carey while he and Watson were still trying to free lifeboat No. 8. "Well, Captain, here's a belt for you," he said. "Get *your* life belt and pay no attention to me," Carey growled. His voice was hoarse and nearly gone, but Duncan understood. He stepped back and did as he was told. Fearing the worst, a handful of No. 8's panic-stricken occupants jumped out, but Carey and Watson didn't give up. As the *Vestris* rolled further and further over, the lifeboat tilted high and dry onto the hull. The officers hopped to the promenade deck railing and stepped gingerly onto the steel plates of the ship's side.

With the sea swirling around their legs, Carey and Watson took advantage of the few seconds the ship had left to cut No. 8 loose. As the boat floated free, its occupants began rowing hard to put distance between themselves and the dying *Vestris*. Sorensen glanced back at the worn-out duo of Carey and Watson. He thought the expression on the captain's face was that of a man who knew he was about to die. Loyal until the very end, Duncan cupped his hands around his mouth and yelled to the captain, "You'd better jump, sir."

"Hell no, you jump," was Carey's reply.

Duncan didn't have to. He simply walked into the waves and began paddling away. Carey and his second officer were left clinging to one another for support when the captain spoke, "My God, my God, I am not to blame for this." Watson was trying to figure out if Carey was talking to him or just mumbling to himself when the captain gave his final order. "Jump, Watson," he croaked, but there wasn't time. The ship's bottom came up suddenly and tossed the men headfirst into the waves.

Cline and Wilma Slaughter were holding hands while they ambled along the deck looking for a boat. "Don't fear, dear," Wilma told her husband. "God will take care of us." The Slaughters rolled off the hull and into the sea. Dozens of others found themselves running for their lives along the keel. Edward Walcott was helping 62-year-old Stewardess Laurinda Moore to the port side rail when they were pitched backward into a pile of deck chairs. As Walcott fought desperately to get free, a wave washed over the deck and he began to feel himself going down with the ship. Moore was gone. As if on a jungle-gym, William Wills Davies hung from a deck rail and looked down to see his feet dangling over the seething water. He lost his grip and dropped ten feet into the sea.

Michael O'Loughlin and two engineers were trying to unfasten poop deck boat No. 12 when they were thrown into the water. Only one engineer came up. O'Loughlin was dead. He was 30-years-old.

Joseph Boxill and another crewman were hanging onto the falls of lifeboat No. 4 when the end came. The two had knives at the ready to cut the ropes, but the order to do so was never given. Now it was too late. They were thrown into the water when the boat tilted onto the hull. Passengers scrambled to get out in a frantic effort to avoid going down with the ship. Keith Burt turned to David Huish and yelled, "We'll have to take our chance." He jumped out of the boat with Huish behind him by half a second. Most of the men were able to climb over the sides, but the women and children weren't as athletic. The unfortunates rode No. 4 to their deaths in the Atlantic.

CHAPTER ELEVEN

"Look, She's Gone"

Like a blue theater curtain, the waves simply closed over the old dancer as she pirouetted into the depths. Paddling nearby, Third Class passenger Carl Schmidt thought the ship's exit was anything but graceful—turning over "like a big potato in a tub of water." Decks that had been horizontal for sixteen years went vertical and then turned upside down. Anything that hadn't slid across them in the previous hours began to free fall to starboard. The contents of the grand saloon, music room, nursery, gymnasium, smoking room, verandah café, cabins and cargo holds came down violently against her bulkheads. Passengers and crew heard a seemingly endless series of crashes and deafening explosions. Above the roar, the deck piano could be heard playing its last disjointed notes as it came unbolted and was smashed to pieces.

Sixty seconds after beginning her death roll, the *Vestris* was gone. A loud gulping sound heralded her descent to the bottom of the ocean. The ship disappeared so suddenly that Marion Batten in No. 8 boat missed everything. She turned away for an instant and by the time she looked back it had vanished. Paul Dana saw a puff of steam come up from the sea where the *Vestris* had been. Only Clytie Raphael spoke, "Look, she's gone."

When the *Vestris* rolled over she threw off anything that wasn't tethered or bolted to her decks. Unused lifeboats and other heavy debris rained down, injuring or killing an untold number of swimmers. Whirlpools swirled everywhere. Dozens thrashed in the water as they groped for anything to hold on to. There were plenty of opportunities. A seemingly unending debris field made up of deck chairs, barrels, hatch covers and woodwork of all types littered the sea in all directions.

Scores of survival dramas began to play out amongst the flotsam: a mother struggled to keep her infant's head above water; newspaper ad salesman Sidney Koppe tried to hang on to a piece of wreckage; Chief Steward Richard Davies untied his life belt and gave it to a woman who was without one. Much like a traffic cop, Second Steward Duncan yelled orders as he treaded water, directing swimmers to the lifeboat nearest them. His shouts were in vain. It was impossible to hear him over the roar of the waves.

After dropping into the sea, Koppe's pal William Wills Davies became one of dozens to be sucked down with the ship. His mind raced as he fought for the surface. Davies thought about what death by drowning would feel like. He'd heard it was an easy way to die, but he didn't want to find out—his wife and three children at home in Queens needed him to survive. Davies finally came up and grabbed a floating chair, but it kept going under. He paddled to a hatch cover and had to give it up as well. Davies ended up clinging to a large beam before finding relative safety on the bottom of an overturned lifeboat. He glanced at his watch. It stopped at 2:31 p.m.

Waves scattered the people who jumped out of lifeboat No. 4 when it was dragged down with the ship. Keith Burt made it to the water in a split-second while David Huish was still scrambling out. The delay saved Huish's life. Suction pulled him down, but he clawed his way back to the surface. Huish grabbed onto a plank and floated while he looked around for a boat—and for his companion. Burt was nowhere to be found. Laundryman James McCulloch made it to the surface, but Margaret McCulloch did not. He screamed his wife's name, but she was gone. Helen Cubbin lost her grip on the children she was caring for. She looked around frantically for any sign of them, but finding none, she began paddling away. For better mobility, Stoker Joseph Boxill ripped off his life belt and also swam from the scene of the wreck.

While holding onto a floating oar, Walcott saw Captain Carey in the water about six feet away. He watched in horror as the despondent commodore bobbed a couple times before slipping beneath the waves for good. Carey never put on a life belt, and once in the water made no attempt to save himself. Walcott was agonizing over having watched the captain die when Stewardess Laurinda Moore paddled up and took the other end of his oar.

Cline and Wilma Slaughter's grip on one another wasn't tight enough to withstand the force of the raging ocean and the couple became separated upon hitting the water. Wilma went under and came up after what seemed like hours. Her hat and shoes gone, she gasped for air as she tried to locate Cline. Miraculously, he was nearby and swimming toward her. She tried paddling in his direction, but the sea of floating junk blocked her way. Cline was within a few yards when a current took hold and began to pull him out of view. Wilma tried pushing through the barrels, chairs and chicken coops to get to him, but she only succeeded in badly scraping her hands. Again and again she screamed for her husband, but Wilma's voice was just another in the legion of swimmers pleading for help. Cline Slaughter was gone.

Second Officer Watson struggled underwater, tangled in a length of rope. Bolts of excruciating pain shot through his chest. Freeing himself, he came up near a pretty young woman struggling to hold onto a floating door. Each time she grabbed on, it popped out of her hands. Watson swam over to help her get a better grip. It was Wilma Slaughter. With no lifeboat in sight, Slaughter's door became a raft for Watson, as well. The pair hung on and rolled on the swells. Despite the fact he was no longer treading water, Watson couldn't catch his breath.

He didn't know it at the time, but he'd broken at least half a dozen ribs. The door turned out to be a special blessing for him, as well. With nothing else to do, Wilma Slaughter began to stare at the sea. The rolling waves had a hypnotic effect. She thought of Cline. She admired the blue of the ocean. As her mind wandered, Wilma Slaughter thought how she would like to one day have a dress of the same color.

When Lionel Licorish looked back to where the ship used to be, he was delighted to see No. 14 boat afloat, just as he'd planned. Licorish swam over and climbed in only to encounter a few oarlocks and a great quantity of seawater. Everything else was gone, and without oars the boat was dead in the water. While he thought about what to do next, Steward Donald Phillips swam up. Licorish pulled him in. A quick look around revealed two oars floating nearby. Licorish jumped out, swam after them and dragged them back to the boat. Moments later, *Vestris* Barber Harry Clevenger and Steward William Millard swam up and were also helped in. No. 14 had a capacity of fifty-three and Licorish was determined to fill every open seat.

Licorish kept the boat in the area and ordered everyone to start bailing. Moments later, he was back in the water—this time to retrieve the boat's sail. When he returned, Refrigerating Engineer Ernest Smith was in the boat. Licorish next fished Purser Pugh and David Huish out of the water. As they rowed around the scene of the wreck, Huish scanned the sea for any sign of his companion, but there was no trace of Keith Burt. Huish prayed he would be found alive.

In the debris field, the human toll of the disaster was making itself apparent in an especially grisly way to injured Storekeeper George Amsdell. As he paddled lamely, Amsdell was horrified to see the body of a child, then another. The victims floated by with ghastly expressions on their faces. In all, the storekeeper saw nine dead bodies, including a handful of children, two women and some shipmates.

Only eight of the *Vestris's* fourteen lifeboats were launched safely. Of the five on the port side, only No. 8 and No. 10 escaped the ship. All five starboard boats made it away, although No. 9 was swamped and barely afloat. Three of the four boats tethered to the poop deck

"LOOK, SHE'S GONE"

survived the sinking. As the afternoon wore on, most of them were leaking miserably. Survivors found themselves bailing and arguing over whether to go back to rescue those still in the water.

A macabre chorus rose up as swimmers screamed desperately for help. Some put their fingers in their mouths and whistled in an effort to get the attention of those in the lifeboats. Carl Schmidt thought they were wasting their breath. In No. 1 boat, Fred Hanson reached for his camera to record the struggle for life, but when he pushed the button nothing happened. He tried again with the same result. With men, women and children drowning all around him, Hanson agonized over his bad luck. He was out of exposures.

There were just over a dozen crew members in No. 7, including Steward Thomas Edwards. Its capacity was sixty-three. Edwards was demanding they row back to rescue swimmers when one of the firemen in the boat decided he'd heard enough. "If you don't shut up, I'll crack you on the head with an oar," he told Edwards. No one stepped up to defend him, so the steward didn't press the issue. A handful of half-drowned passengers were plucked from the water, but the paltry rescue effort was nothing like the one Edwards had hoped for.

Lifeboat No. 13 launched itself by floating off the poop deck when the ship rolled over. Boatswain's Mates John Myrick and Archibald Bannister swam up, climbed in and began rowing. They quickly picked up four crewmen and Carlos Quiros. The diplomat and anyone else who wasn't at the oars immediately began bailing to keep the boat afloat. As Quiros worked, one of the Barbadian sailors slipped and accidentally kicked him in the shin. A livid Quiros cursed the man out loud. "Naw man, don't swear just now," the sailor cautioned. "Please man, don't swear." Despite their fears of ramming into floating wreckage and holing their boat, the men cruised around and plucked fifteen more swimmers from the water, including fugitive passenger Ovelton Maxey, Second Steward Duncan and Chief Engineer Adams.

In another part of the debris field, the men in crowded No. 10 were also bailing for their lives. The seasick Dr. Lehner could only vomit and wasn't much help. It didn't matter. Despite the frantic effort, there were always six inches of water in the bottom of the boat. Grief added to their frustration. Fred Puppe watched No. 4 boat go down with the ship. He had no way of knowing whether his wife and baby were among those carried to their deaths, but he had a strong feeling they were. Puppe had no choice but to keep at his job despite his anguish.

Before long, nearly-empty lifeboat No. 3 came near and allowed some of bloated No. 10's occupants to transfer off. Dr. Lehner and William Burke did so and found themselves bailing out yet another leaky boat. When the transfers were complete, the men of No. 3 caught sight of swamped No. 9 wallowing nearby and called out to its occupants to swim for it. Chief Officer Johnson and a handful of crewmen did and were pulled aboard, but three others wouldn't budge. Despite repeated shouts of encouragement, they didn't even try. The men were never seen again. Johnson took command of No. 3 and examined the dozen flares it carried. He found many of them to be rotten and unusable. Further inspection of the supplies revealed a host of other problems. The bottom of the lantern was missing, rendering it useless. In addition, there was no fresh water and the boat's tiller was broken. The state of affairs was a far cry from the inspector's recent pronouncement the boats were fully equipped.

Cline Slaughter spent the hours after he lost sight of his wife swimming from one piece of wreckage to another. During that time he was passed by four boats. Slaughter was eventually rescued by lifeboat No. 10 at dusk. Wilma and Second Officer Watson were saved by No. 11. Someone wrapped the exhausted redhead in an overcoat and she laid down in the bottom of the boat. Cline and Wilma Slaughter were each unaware the other was alive and well.

CHAPTER TWELVE

"We Don't Want No Women In Here"

Lifeboat No. 8 began leaking as soon as it hit the water. Men immediately took to either rowing or bailing. Those without pails used their hats to throw water out. Anne Devore, Marion Batten and the other women crouched in the bottom of the boat in an effort to keep out of the way. Although the situation was serious, the lifeboats were designed with such a crisis in mind. Attached under the benches were steel air tanks that could keep them afloat if and when they ever became swamped. For now, the tanks weren't needed—the bailing was keeping ahead of the incoming seawater. With no officer aboard, Sorensen took command.

One of the little boys started to whimper and his mother comforted him. A few women cried softly, but for the most part passengers remained calm. No. 8 strained under the weight of its human cargo, but there was hope. Nine other lifeboats were in the immediate vicinity and could easily come to the rescue, if needed. Moments after the *Vestris* went down one of them paddled by with just a handful of crew aboard. Someone yelled to the men in the near-empty lifeboat to let some passengers transfer over, but Sorensen waved them off. "Never mind," he yelled. "Go and pick up some of those people in the water." Sorensen was confident the air tanks would keep them afloat until everyone was plucked out of the sea and he had no reason to believe otherwise. Unfortunately, not long after the boat rowed away, the fates of every man, woman and child in No. 8 were sealed. The tin strip nailed to the lifeboat's side in the half-hearted attempt to patch the gash worked itself loose and came off. Water began to flow in at an alarming rate. Norman Batten yelled to the bailers to keep going, but it was no use.

However, as Sorensen predicted, the people in No. 8 weren't alone for long. Within a few minutes swamped No. 9 came near, but the handful of men in it couldn't offer any help as their own boat was floating on air tanks. Spirits were buoyed moments later when lifeboat No. 1 came along. No. 8's occupants could see from the white jackets the men were wearing that *Vestris* stewards were aboard. Convinced rescue was at hand, the passengers cried out. To their great relief, No. 1 rowed closer and closer until the gap between the two boats was only a couple of feet. Earl Devore urged his wife to try for it and Anne hopped across with Speedway Lady. They made it easily. Marion Batten was about to do the same when a Barbadian crewman in No. 1 called an end to the rescue operation. "We can't take any more," he said. "We've got to pick up survivors." An incredulous Batten was straddling the sea with a foot in each boat when the end of an oar was pressed against her chest and she was abruptly shoved back into No. 8. "We don't want no more women in here," another sailor yelled. With that, No. 1 boat began to row away.

Seawater was now pouring into No. 8 faster than it could be bailed out. Panic began to set in despite the pleas of Sorensen and Norman Batten to remain calm. Sorensen knew the lifeboat would sink sooner rather than later, but he didn't share the information for fear of causing any further commotion. Besides, there was no reason why they still couldn't be saved by one of the other boats. The men of No. 8 tried rowing toward some of them, but on more than one occasion, as their own occupants saw the swamped and crowded boat coming closer, they pulled in the opposite direction. Sadly, No. 8's exhausted passengers were in no condition to mount a serious chase. The boat was almost full of water, but they somehow found the energy to battle close to No. 1 once more. Some of the women rose to their feet to yell for help. One of them held her little boy up for the men in No. 1 to see. "Please come and save us," she shrieked. There was no reaction. The men in the near-empty boat stared blankly back at them. "Help, we are sinking," Earl Devore roared. From her seat in No. 1, Anne Devore could make out her husband's voice in the chorus of people begging for rescue.

Sorensen's mind raced. He wanted the crewmen in No. 1 to at least take the women and children off and let the men cling to their lifelines. He wished he had a gun to shoot one of them. Sorensen believed if he did, the others would change their minds and bring their boat alongside. His hopes were dashed despite the fact he had an ally in No. 1. The desperate men and women could see Anne Devore gesticulating as she harangued her boat mates, "For God's sake go and get them!"

"Sit down, we can't stop!" a sailor commanded.

"Cowards!" she shot back.

At last they could take no more and the race car driver's wife was told to sit down and shut up. Devore wilted into the bottom of the boat where she wouldn't have to watch her husband and friends die. As she hugged Speedway Lady close, the men at the oars began rowing away.

Soon after abandoning Earl Devore and the others, the men of No. 1 were presented with a chance to, at least partially, atone for their colossal wrong. At a distance, they could see a man clinging to an overturned boat with one arm and waving at them with the other. The fiery Devore heard his cries and came back with a vengeance to plead for his life. "You wouldn't leave a man there to perish?" she asked. They were left with another decision to make. The man continued to yell for help while the boat's occupants coolly discussed whether or not to go and get him. Finally, they agreed to row close enough to give him a chance to swim for it while staying far enough away to avoid ramming any large pieces of wreckage and holing their boat. If he could make it, they would help him aboard. Lifeboat No. 1's occupants rowed nearer and nearer to the man and stopped when they were about twenty feet away. They watched the castaway shed his overcoat and begin swimming. As he paddled, the man could feel himself starting to cramp up, but he made it close enough for a crewman to extend a boat hook. It was William Wills Davies. He climbed in and sat down next to Devore. "You know you're mighty lucky to have been picked up," Devore said to him. "The Negroes didn't want to do it, but most of us insisted."

Those aboard No. 1 were able to make out the sight of a swamped boat in the distance. Men and women could clearly be seen struggling in the water around it. Devore was sure it was lifeboat No. 8. "For God's sake, go after them," Devore raged. "I'm sure my husband is in that boat!" The debate began anew. Some wanted to attempt a rescue, while others argued that if they did, their own boat would be swamped under the additional weight. No decision was ever really made. Instead, those at the oars simply began to row away. "You ought to be ashamed of yourselves, leaving men to die like that," Devore screamed. This time no one ordered her to be silent. It was easier to simply ignore her. Devore turned to Davies and asked, "What do you think of their leaving people to perish?" Her voice was purposely loud enough for all to hear. Davies also tried making the case for a rescue attempt, but there was no real desire to go back. The rowers put more and more distance between themselves and the swamped lifeboat. First Officer Bolger's decision to stay out of No. 1 had come back to haunt the survivors. There was no officer in command and the absence of leadership was costing people their lives.

Just after 4:00 p.m., the clouds cleared to reveal a bright red sunset. However, thunderheads soon returned and the skies opened again. The driving rain was accompanied by hail, lightning and booming thunderclaps. The bad weather would continue on and off throughout the night. Like a tortoise, William Wills Davies tried retracting his head and shoulders into his life belt to keep warm, but it didn't really work. Between storms the wind would dry his clothes, but the rain would come back only to soak them again. He thought he would go mad. During one lull, the people in No. 1 put a sea anchor over the side and huddled together in an effort to keep warm. When it came to enduring the harsh weather, swimmers actually had the advantage. The water's temperature of nearly eighty degrees sustained them throughout the night.

In No. 13 boat, Quiros, Chief Engineer Adams and the others began to wonder if they would ever be saved. Every so often someone shouted for help, but lone voices were easily drowned out by the roaring ocean. Finally, someone began counting "One, two, three," and everyone yelled in unison, "Help!" Regrettably, no rescue ships heard their cries. The castaways began to see what they thought were searchlights in nearly every direction, causing them to row toward each in vain attempts to reach the closest one. A sailor started lighting flares to attract the attention of the rescue ships, but with the boat shipping water at an alarming rate, a forlorn Quiros began to pray.

On board the *American Shipper*, Captain Cumings sent a message to his counterpart on the *Ohio Maru*: "Have you seen *Vestris* and do you need our assistance to accommodate rescued?" There was no response. The Japanese ship had been only fifty miles away from the coordinates given by O'Loughlin and it should have arrived in the vicinity of the sinking by evening. Cumings knew if she were on scene, there was no question she would have encountered at least some debris and possibly even lifeboats full of survivors. The *Maru's* captain should have radioed an update by now. As the *Shipper* made full speed to the scene of the wreck, Cumings began to believe he *would* make it in time to save lives.

CHAPTER THIRTEEN

"I've Got to Give Up"

Fred Sorensen was watching lifeboat No. 1 in the distance when a wave washed him and a handful of others into the sea. As the current pulled him away, Sorensen thought of the passengers still in No. 8, and how in a strange way he was glad he wouldn't be around to see them drown. He looked back one last time and saw the men and women standing huddled together in the swamped lifeboat. Sorensen thought they looked like a little island of people in the sea.

As he began to swim, Sorensen noticed Stewardess Clara Ball and First Class passenger Herman Rueckert struggling nearby. Glancing ahead, he spotted a boat about a quarter of a mile away. He decided to try for it. Sorensen looked back again and saw Rueckert, but not Ball. The German was doing a surprisingly good job of keeping up. As the pair swam closer, the lifeboat they had hoped would be their salvation began to row away from them. The prospect of being left to drown yet again was too much for the choking Rueckert. He sputtered at Sorensen, "I've got to give up."

"I'VE GOT TO GIVE UP"

At that moment the men noticed yet another lifeboat nearby—this one under sail. Sorensen thought it had been sent from heaven. "Don't give up," he commanded Rueckert. "I'm going to swim as fast as I can and see if I can head him off." A lifetime of swimming had prepared him for this moment. Sorensen picked an angle that would put him in line to meet up with the boat and battled the waves and the swirling current to swim close enough for its occupants to see him. At last, Sorensen saw the sail begin to come down as they prepared to pluck him from the sea. As soon as he was hauled aboard, Sorensen told the boat's commander, Quartermaster Lionel Licorish, where to find the dog paddling German.

After Rueckert was saved, Sorensen demanded they go back for the others. A search for Ball came up empty, so the men tried making their way to the place where Sorensen had last seen No. 8. Night fell while the boat attempted to beat its way back against the wind. Licorish had to steer with an oar, as there was no rudder. As the lifeboat reached the crest of each wave, Sorensen could still see the people standing in what was left of No. 8. In the end, the strong winds and high seas were too much. No. 14 lacked the power to reach them. Exhausted, the men gave it up. Sorensen was livid. He knew everyone could have been saved by lifeboat No. 1. The bitterness he felt toward the men aboard her would be with him the rest of his life.

Paul Dana and the others hung on as wave after wave pounded lifeboat No. 8 mercilessly. From Dana's point of view, they seemed a hundred feet high. It wasn't long before the swamped boat began to sink. Clytie Raphael spoke again, "Oh my God, the lifeboat's leaving us." A large wave crashed down, flipped the boat and spilled everyone into the sea. The lifeboat came down hard on Dana's neck and trapped him underneath. As he struggled to get out from under No. 8, he saw a woman's foot pop out of the water. Dana grabbed it and pulled Clara Ball out with him. After coming up, Dana glanced around and was relieved to discover nearly everyone else survived the capsizing, including the children. However, when he counted to be sure, he came up one woman short. Raphael was gone. Those remaining pulled together, flipped the boat over and climbed in again. It was the first of half a dozen or so times the scene repeated, with fewer and fewer people coming up each time No. 8 capsized. The children were the first to disappear, followed by most of the women.

The air tanks Sorensen once counted on to keep No. 8 afloat were coming loose as waves hammered the boat to pieces. In addition, so many of the original occupants had been washed out, there weren't enough people left to flip the boat over anymore. It was floating upside down, with its air tanks keeping only the bow out of the water. Those remaining held on to the sides. Stoker Gerald Burton became their leader. "Stay with me, and I won't let you drown," he yelled.

After coming to the realization it was only a matter of time before his charges slipped away, Burton decided to take life belts off nearby corpses and put them to better use. There were so many bodies in the area Burton was able to collect several. When his arms were full, he swam back to overturned No. 8 and fashioned them into a raft for the Battens and Third Class passenger Mary Ulrich. Once everyone was relatively safe on the makeshift raft, there was nothing left for Burton and Stoker John Morris to do but hang on, tread water and watch what they thought were the searchlights of rescue ships playing on the waves.

Norman Batten was so exhausted from bailing and flipping the boat over he had become delirious, but Marion did her best to keep his spirits up. She was all smiles despite the ordeal, keeping the conversation going and the mood light. Suddenly, the group was illuminated by the beam of a searchlight. They were sure they had been spotted, but they were dead wrong.

A handful of others who were washed off of No. 8 came together on yet another raft improvised from life preservers and bits of wreckage. Major Inouye and his wife Teruko, Elvira Rua and Third Class passenger Dolores Doril would cling to the raft and one another while they waited for rescue. The wreckage that was lifeboat No. 8 was abandoned.

"I'VE GOT TO GIVE UP"

Meanwhile, the occupants of No. 1 boat passed the hours by cheerfully estimating when they would be rescued. Waiter Thomas Griffin said he was sure they'd be picked up soon—around two or three in the morning—and then he checked his watch. It was only 9:00 p.m. Devore shared her worst fears with Davies—that her husband was dead, but she didn't let on to the others. Like her friend Marion Batten, Devore kept a positive attitude, even going so far as to cheer the men while they rowed.

S.S. American Shipper. (U.S. Shipping Board)

After making top speed for hours, the *American Shipper* arrived at the position reported by the New York shore stations at 7:30 p.m., but no trace of the *Vestris* or her lifeboats was found. Cumings faced a dilemma. The Brooklyn Navy Yard's coordinates were a full thirty miles north of the position given by Captain Carey and the stations at Cape May, New Jersey and Bethany Beach, Delaware. Finding anyone alive over such a wide area would require great patience and a feat of extraordinary seamanship. Fortunately, the captain was up to the challenge. Cumings charted a course through all the positions he'd plotted and doubled his lookouts.

LAST DANCE OF THE VESTRIS

At 10:15 p.m., the *Shipper* arrived at the position transmitted by the *Vestris* herself. Cumings slowed his ship. Searchlights swept the waves. Lookouts strained their eyes and ears for signs of life. One man sighted a white light, but it turned out to be the masthead light of another rescue ship. The S*hipper* searched the area until 2:00 a.m. Tuesday, but there was still no trace of her. Wireless messages began to trickle in from other vessels reporting they were also struggling to find any sign of the *Vestris*.

As the hours wore on, the strain on the crews of the rescue ships became greater. Dr. Bowlen and some other *Shipper* crew members began to lose hope, but not Cumings. The skipper checked and rechecked the positions given by the *Vestris* and the shore stations before deciding to expand the search area. For the next few hours the *Shipper* steamed west of the *Vestris's* reported position, then south and east again.

CHAPTER FOURTEEN

"Take Hold of One End, and I'll Take the Other"

Paul Dana had seen enough suffering, so when he saw a large piece of wreckage floating by, he decided to take his chances and abandon the deathtrap that was lifeboat No. 8. He invited a fellow castaway to join him. "Come on," he yelled. Dana swam to a wood beam and Stewardess Clara Ball followed without a word. As it turned out, Ball didn't go with Sorensen when he swam away from No. 8 and instead paddled back to the boat. This time would be different. "Take hold of one end," he instructed. "And I'll take the other." She did. The life belts Dana and Ball wore barely kept their heads above water as they were battered by the waves. Again and again, the pair endured the harrowing split-second after each crashed down when it felt like they would be smothered by the foam.

As time passed, the ocean's rage tested their will to live. Dana could barely maintain his grip on the splintered beam because his hands were being cut to pieces. Ball was wearing gloves and didn't have the problem. The pair decided to conserve as much energy as possible by avoiding unnecessary movement, but in the stormy sea it was a tall order. Dana took his first long, hard look at Ball and noticed something strange about her appearance. "What in the world is that you have stuck in the front of your life preserver?" he asked. Ball's blue eyes twinkled as she gave Dana a big smile and pulled out a high-heeled shoe. "Aren't they pretty?" she asked. As they floated in the middle of the Atlantic, surrounded by death, Clara Ball told Paul Dana about the difficulties she encountered while shopping for footwear in New York. She explained how her narrow feet made it next to impossible to find shoes that fit properly and she wanted to be sure her good pair was saved when she left the *Vestris*.

The duo knew lifeboats were nearby. Every so often one of them would yell for help, but there was no way people in boats could hear their voices over the sound of the roaring sea. Ball adjusted her grip on the spar as clouds again began to cover the sky. Paul Dana and Clara Ball eventually began what would become a very long conversation. Ball told Dana she was one of the *Vestris's* two stewardesses. Until she mentioned it, he had no idea who his fellow castaway even was. As Dana chatted and kicked his legs in the warm water, his mind turned to the subject of sharks. He didn't let on to Ball, but he couldn't stop thinking about what it would feel like to be attacked by one. It was driving him mad. Every so often, Dana felt a fish brush against his side. He squirmed but said nothing for fear of upsetting Ball. If she were also thinking of sharks, she kept it to herself as well.

The conversation continued with Dana and Ball comparing notes and reconstructing the disaster's time line. She told him she'd heard the rumor an SOS went out at 8:00 a.m. Monday but was later canceled by Carey. Dana said the captain probably thought the *Vestris* would recover, but he cursed him anyway. So did Ball. Several hours and thousands of words later, the two came to the conclusion that the sinking had been "a tough break" for the old man.

In the early morning hours, the pair's spirits were buoyed by what they thought were signs of life. Dana and Ball joined the countless others who were passing the time by watching searchlights scan the ocean. They knew there was no way any rescue ship's lookouts could see them at such a great distance, but the lights' presence gave them hope they would eventually be saved. Unfortunately, all were mistaken. The searchlights didn't belong to ships at all. They were actually watching flashes of lightning illuminate the sky.

Stoker Joseph Boxill was still swimming from crate to crate when he came upon a fellow crewman lying on a large piece of wreckage. He thought he recognized the man as "Slim," the engineers' steward. Boxill joined him and the two floated together until they saw another man resting on an even bigger piece of debris. "Let's swim over to that thing," Boxill said. Slim couldn't swim, so the stoker slipped into the water and towed him toward the wreckage. Once there, they discovered the man clinging to it was a passenger. The trio wouldn't be together long. "Slim" suffered a cramp, let go and drifted off into the darkness. Soon after, the passenger floated away, leaving Boxill exhausted and alone. He never asked either man's name. Boxill was about to give himself up for dead when he saw something that cheered him. A red flare could be seen high in the night sky. It seemed a million miles away, but he took comfort in knowing others were alive and nearby. Boxill watched the flares for awhile and dreamed of rescue. Then he blacked out.

Captain Cumings was rewarded for his persistence when, just before 4:00 a.m., the *American Shipper's* lookouts sighted a flare dead ahead. Passengers who had been up all night received the payoff they had been waiting for—the rescue was finally underway. Lifeboat No. 5 under the command of Third Officer Welland battled the heavy wind, rain and lightning and within minutes, bumped against the hull. *Shipper* sailors tied it up and helped the weary survivors aboard as fast as they could, where once on deck, each was wrapped in a blanket and handed a hot cup of coffee or soup. The well-dressed passengers of the *American Shipper* watched as the haggard castaways appeared one by one. Former Second Class passenger Helen Cubbin was too weak to climb and had to be hauled aboard in a cargo net. No one cheered, as the situation was tense and the mood somber. When No. 5 was lowered from the *Vestris*, there were only a few crewmen aboard. Now, thirty-seven survivors were being taken off including Cubbin, Welland, Steward Hogg and Storekeeper Amsdell. Only a few were passengers. No children were seen. The boat could have held sixty-three.

Rough seas and high winds complicated the rescues, but the physical condition of the survivors made the work especially challenging. Many of them had broken bones, while others suffered from exposure and shock from long hours spent in the water. Those who were able to climb used rope ladders; the weak and injured were hauled up in cargo nets.

The crew of the *S.S. Berlin* also passed a long and difficult night. In a pessimistic wireless message, Captain Eric von Thulen expressed doubts he'd find anyone alive: "Very strong Northerly winds blowing, which is no kind of weather for men, women and children already weakened by a day and a half in small boats or clinging to wave-washed rafts." Even so, the Germans would persist. *Berlin* passengers and crew knew they were getting close to the wreck scene when they began to see crushed lifeboats, unused life belts and other debris float by. It wasn't long before the *American Shipper* came into view.

Half an hour after No. 5 was picked up, sailors aboard the *American Shipper* heard cries in the water. The beam of the ship's searchlight soon revealed another lifeboat. The survivors in No. 1 were out of flares and yelling for help when they were spotted. Anne Devore and Speedway Lady, William Wills Davies, Fred Hanson, Carpenter Wohld and fifteen others joined the *Vestris* complement on board the *Shipper*. Devore prayed her husband made it to another boat.

The French oil tanker *Myriam* picked up lifeboat No. 11, under the command of Second Officer Watson, at about 4:30 a.m. Most of the thirty-five aboard the lifeboat were crew, but a handful of passengers were also saved. Upon being helped aboard, an embarrassed Wilma Slaughter discovered her dress had shrunk into what she thought was an all too revealing "French creation." Ironically, it would take a Frenchman to solve the problem. Captain Fernandez Forey provided her with the latest in men's shipboard fashion—an undershirt, a pair of

"TAKE HOLD OF ONE END, AND I'LL TAKE THE OTHER"

his own white trousers, an overcoat and a cap. Ever the gentleman, Forey also gave Slaughter the use of his cabin. It was there she would wait for news of her husband and on Wednesday, November 14, celebrate her twenty-first birthday.

The rescues continued when lookouts sighted a flare from No. 3 boat, under the command of Chief Officer Johnson. At 5:15 a.m., the *American Shipper* pulled alongside. The lifeboat made it away from the *Vestris* with only eleven crewmen aboard, but they were especially active at the disaster scene. The men fished twenty-seven people out of the water, including Edward Walcott, his oar-mate Laurinda Moore and Herbert Johnston. They also took some survivors off jam-packed No. 10. A total of forty-five were aboard, making No. 3 boat among the most full of the *Vestris's* tragic fleet. However, as the steady stream of castaways came aboard, a disturbing pattern was becoming apparent. Only five survivors were passengers.

From 5:30 a.m. until daybreak nothing further was seen, but when the sun came out lookouts spotted lifeboats No. 10 and No. 14. It took three attempts to maneuver the *Shipper* close enough to begin rescue operations, but within two hours the occupants of both were safely aboard. While the work was in progress, *Shipper* lookouts reported another lifeboat paddling nearby. Cumings radioed von Thulen to ask if the *Berlin* could retrieve it.

Little did the two skippers know, their vessels had already been seen by the men in lifeboat No. 13, prompting a lively discussion to break out on board. The survivors estimated the vessels were about ten miles away, with the ship that would turn out to be the *American Shipper* being slightly closer. The men at the oars rowed toward it, but after getting close enough to determine that one vessel looked more like a cargo ship and the other an ocean liner, Carlos Quiros began to make the case to change direction. "Better make for the other one," he advised. "Chances are we shall have a better meal there." The prospect of superior food won out and the men pulled for the bigger ship. The *Berlin* slowed and stopped to haul No. 13's complement of five passengers and eighteen crewmen aboard.

LAST DANCE OF THE VESTRIS

The diplomat turned out to be right about the level of service aboard the liner. The smiling men were photographed in one of the *Berlin's* dining rooms enjoying a hearty breakfast moments after being rescued. Passengers who watched the rescue stayed up while their ship cruised around to look for more survivors. There was no way anyone was going to bed.

No. 14 boat comes alongside the *American Shipper*. (U.S. Shipping Board)

Once he was safely aboard the *Shipper*, Chief Officer Johnson joined Cumings on the bridge to discuss the fate of the *Vestris's* lifeboats. Johnson reconstructed the disaster from memory in order to determine how many of them made it away from the ship. He also reported a raft floating nearby. Cumings warned the other ships to be on the lookout: "Chief Officer of *Vestris* very much concerned about a life raft have just passed a hatch should think it was near here."

The *Myriam* made the next rescue, picking up lifeboat No. 7 with just over twenty people aboard, including Marconi men Verchere and MacDonald. After spending several more hours in the area and finding nothing, Captain Forey sent a wireless message to announce he was calling off his search: "Arrived at scene of *Vestris* disaster at 2 a.m. I have saved 54 people. Having searched fruitlessly I am leaving and proceeding to New York with the rescued people." Of the dozens of survivors the *Myriam* picked up, only eight were passengers, with Wilma Slaughter being the only woman saved. No children were among the rescued.

After reviewing the chain of events with Johnson and communicating with the other rescue ships, Captain Cumings came to believe that all lifeboats that made it away from the *Vestris* were accounted for. Even so, he decided to continue the search for rafts and swimmers. For the rest of the morning, the *Shipper* moved carefully through the debris field. As the weather began to clear, passengers and crew saw wreckage and more than a dozen corpses in the water. The ship didn't stop to pick them up, as Cumings wanted to conserve precious resources for anyone still alive on the choppy seas. Some *Shipper* passengers scanning the waves for survivors recoiled in horror when they witnessed a shark gnawing at the arm of one dead man. They also saw one of the most heart-rending sights of the entire operation. The bodies of two little boys floated by—one of them about four years of age, the other about eight. The scenes were so gruesome a former army nurse said they eclipsed the horrors she witnessed during the Great War.

Meanwhile, Dr. Bowlen and his volunteer nurses were busy caring for the dozens of survivors in need of medical attention. About forty required treatment for injuries ranging from scrapes and scratches to broken bones. Second Cook Ernest Carpenter had a broken leg. Seaman Reginald Bannister's foot was badly cut. So were the hands of Pantryman Jean Gladianes—injured when the steel beam dropped into lifeboat No. 4. Purser Pugh's back was sprained. In addition, both of Steward Hogg's broken arms had to be set. Bowlen treated Stewardess Laurinda Moore for shock, Davies for bronchitis and shock and Walcott for broken ribs. The doctor also removed two fingers from the left hand of Third Class passenger Lloyd Keiser. They had been so badly crushed against the *Vestris's* side they couldn't be saved.

Bowlen's prescription for most survivors was bed rest—if a bed could be found. Despite the best efforts of *American Shipper* passengers to double up, there still weren't enough berths for everyone. Some

LAST DANCE OF THE VESTRIS

survivors slept in public rooms while others stretched out in passageways. It was impossible to walk around without stumbling over sleeping *Vestris* passengers and crew.

Once they had been lifted to safety, the rescued had different priorities. Former Second Class passenger Alfredo Ramos lamented the destruction of his white shirt. The dye from his red necktie bled and ruined it. Edward Marvin cut off a piece of his life belt as a souvenir for his children. Reporter Davies sat down to pen his account for his newspaper. William Adams went straight for the wireless office to let loved ones know he made it: "Arrive New York probably Wednesday afternoon. Dr. A. Groman of Odebolt, Iowa and myself both safe on *American Shipper* and absolutely well."

Vestris survivors in lifeboat No. 13 prepare to board the *Berlin*. (*U.S. Shipping Board*)

"TAKE HOLD OF ONE END, AND I'LL TAKE THE OTHER"

Vestris Hospital Attendant Hugh Jones, Pantryman Jean Gladianes and Steward George Hogg enjoy a smoke on the deck of the *American Shipper* after being treated for their injuries. (*Associated Press*)

For those on Fireman Gerald Burton's makeshift raft, prayer had replaced conversation. Their situation was grave. Norman Batten was exhausted and had slipped into delirium. Every so often, he tried to hold onto his wife by grabbing at her hair. Each time, Marion Batten patiently freed herself and readjusted her grip on her husband. Marion thought her prayers were answered when, through the haze, two ships came into view. Burton tied a piece of cloth to the end of an oar and waved it frantically in a bid to attract the lookouts' attention when hope turned to horror. A large wave broke on the raft and Marion lost her grip on Norman. The race car driver used his last drop of energy to clutch at his wife, but the surging water ripped him from her arms. There was nothing either one could have done. Norman Batten floated away face down, powerless to save himself. Marion, who for years watched her husband cheat death from behind the wheel of his speedy race car, now watched him drown slowly in the Atlantic Ocean. The ships were too far away to offer any help. Marion Batten would languish in the water for hours more.

At 8:00 a.m. the dreadnought battleship *U.S.S. Wyoming* steamed into the area and made contact with the *Myriam* and *American Shipper*. Cumings and Forey reported to the warship's commanding officers, Captain Luther Overstreet and Vice Admiral Montgomery Taylor, that all but two of the *Vestris's* lifeboats made it away from the ship and advised that two others were missing and believed lost. Overstreet determined the debris field would not have drifted as far as a lifeboat would have, so he ordered the *Wyoming's* course altered. It proved to be a smart call.

Lookouts rang the battleship's bridge to report wreckage in the water. As the vessel steamed closer and closer, the body of a man could be seen lying on a floating hatch cover. Overstreet maneuvered his ship in such a way that the castaway would be sheltered from the high winds under the bow. A cheer went up among the crew when a strong-armed sailor tossed a line and hit the castaway in the chest, but the voices went silent when he didn't move. A crewman lowered over the side discovered an unconscious Joseph Boxill. The stoker was hauled aboard.

After watching her husband drown, Marion Batten felt like she couldn't go on. She whispered another prayer, "If help is coming, send it quickly, God." Her petition was granted seemingly on cue when the *Wyoming* steamed into view. The now re-energized group of Batten, Mary Ulrich, Gerald Burton and John Morris waved their oar-flag once more, but they ultimately threw it aside to try for the ship. Although physically exhausted and emotionally traumatized, Batten abandoned the raft and began to swim for her life. Burton helped the women paddle toward the ship while Morris swam alongside.

It wasn't long before the *Wyoming's* lookouts reported an ocean teeming with bodies. A few men and women were seen swimming some distance in front of the ship while a handful of others floated on what looked like an improvised raft. Overstreet moved to rescue the swimmers first. Marion Batten, Mary Ulrich, John Morris and Burton were safe at last. The stoker made good on his promise.

Captain Overstreet next lowered a powered boat to retrieve the group on the raft. From a distance it looked like there were four people clinging to it, but upon pulling alongside sailors made a grim discovery. Only Dolores Doril, Elvira Rua and Teruko Inouye were alive. The fourth was the lifeless body of Major Inouye, who had succumbed to exhaustion and exposure during the night. His distraught wife had been clinging to it for hours. One by one, the survivors were hauled into the boat without incident except for Madame Inouye, who tried desperately to convince her rescuers to leave her to die with her husband. Sailors had to pry Major Inouye's corpse from his wife's arms before it could be set adrift. They also had to restrain the hysterical widow from jumping out to swim after him. The boat began making its way back to the ship as the Major's body was carried away by the current.

Paul Dana and Clara Ball were hoping for a quick end to their ordeal, but as the day dawned there wasn't a ship in view. Their situation was becoming more desperate as the morning wore on. The spar that had buoyed them throughout the stormy night was beginning to come apart. Dana and Ball now had the nearly impossible task of holding the wreckage together while using it for support at the same time. Dana's hands were cut to pieces, but Ball's gloves made the job a bit easier for her. The pair was also having trouble seeing, as their eyes, crusty with salt, were burning badly. They were starving, thirsty and exhausted, but they refused to give up. As a young Doughboy, Dana lived through the nightmare that was the Great War. He was determined to survive in the waters of the Gulf Stream.

Their stubbornness was rewarded about mid-morning when Dana saw a ship on the horizon he estimated to be about twenty miles away. With their spar nearly gone, he suggested the obvious. "How about it," he asked. "Shall we swim for it?" The odds of making it seemed insurmountable, but the alternative was certain death. Without a word, the stewardess let go and started to paddle. Dana swam next to her.

When they had been swimming for an hour and the ship didn't seem any closer, Dana glanced back over his shoulder. To his utter amazement, he saw another vessel about a mile behind them steaming in their direction. It appeared as though her lookouts had seen them, so Dana stopped swimming, ripped off his shirttail and waved it in the air to make sure they did.

Cumings maneuvered the *American Shipper* as close to the swimmers as was safely possible and asked for volunteers to crew the boat that would go get them. Nearly every sailor stepped forward. Second Officer Ed Ohman selected eight and the men hopped in a lifeboat. A relieved Dana and Ball watched it being lowered, but the pair would have to cheat death again if they were to survive. The danger came in the form of the rescue ship itself. The *Shipper* was stopped, but drifting ominously in their direction. Unless the lifeboat plucked them out of the water in short order, Dana and Ball would be crushed to death. The sailors also had to contend with unstable and choppy waves that seemed to be coming from and going everywhere. The "confused sea" would make the rescue an even greater challenge for the men.

Precious seconds ticked away as the lifeboat's crew battled to get into a position where they could haul the pair aboard. It would be a close shave. As the steamer drifted closer and closer, sailors finally rowed near enough for the smiling Ohman to throw Dana a line. Dana grabbed the rope, tied it around his body and held onto Ball as he was hauled in. "Take the man up first," Ball said when their boat came alongside the big ship. "I can go up the ladder." She was being overly optimistic. After eighteen hours in the water, neither Dana nor Ball had the strength to climb. Instead, sailors aboard the *American Shipper* lowered a cargo net and hoisted both of them up.

Once on deck, Ball had enough energy to turn down the offer of a chair. "Thank you, but I am well enough to stand," she said. Someone asked if she was scared when the *Vestris* went down. "Well," the stewardess said. "You can't be afraid when you have got to keep your head." After treating Ball, Dr. Bowlen ripped off Dana's wet clothes and gave him a thorough examination. Bowlen prescribed two shots of whiskey and Dana was escorted to a cabin, where he promptly fell into a deep sleep.

Once Dana and Ball were aboard, Cumings ordered Ohman and his men to cast off once more to check the dozen or so bodies floating nearby for signs of life. None were found. The wind freshened and the seas began to pick up as the boat paddled back. Cumings chose not to risk any more lives in what would now be the treacherous job of hoisting the boat back on deck. After his men had climbed back aboard, the captain ordered it set adrift. Cumings next had to decide whether to keep his ship in the area. The possibility of rescuing more swimmers was a compelling reason to stay, but he was also mindful of those who needed more serious medical attention than Dr. Bowlen could give. Satisfied any remaining survivors would be picked up by the flotilla of government ships now in the vicinity, the captain fired off a wireless message before turning his vessel toward home: "Fuel getting low must start for New York. Chief Officer and Third Officer agree that only eight boats succeeded in getting away from *Vestris*. We picked two people out of water. Hope you succeed in further rescues. Cumings."

In a message summing up the rescue operation, Cumings inadvertently coined a phrase that would instantly create two heroes for the millions of people awaiting details from the disaster scene: "Rescued five boats, all aboard at 7:30. Steamed through wreckage, found man and woman in water. Launched boat and picked up two pluckiest people ever met." Newsmen listening in on the dots and dashes intercepted the message and the Pluckiest Pair was born. Reporters immediately began hatching plans to obtain interviews with the couple who floated together in the shark-infested Atlantic Ocean for nearly a day—and survived. Amazingly, they weren't the last *Vestris* castaways to be picked up.

Third Class passenger Carl Schmidt was desperate. It was almost noon and he was still swimming for his life; his neck and shoulders badly chafed and bruised by his rough, waterlogged lifebelt. The odds the Chicago blacksmith would survive were remote, but his situation was actually improving. After spending hours in a saltwater-induced stupor, he could feel his mind beginning to come back to life. It couldn't have picked a better time to do so. As he awakened, Schmidt noticed what looked like a far-off ship zigzagging in his direction. He was overcome with joy, but at the same time he was terrified at the possibility it would steam past without noticing him. As the vessel came closer, Schmidt waved his arms frantically. After several minutes of waving without being acknowledged, he felt his "heart grow colder" than the water in which he floated.

The Pluckiest Pair, Paul Dana and Clara Ball. (*Wide World*)

"TAKE HOLD OF ONE END, AND I'LL TAKE THE OTHER"

On board the *Berlin,* lookouts rang the bridge to report seeing someone in the water wearing a gray cap. The captain commanded sailors to alert the man he'd been spotted and signaled his engineers for "full stop," but the *Berlin* was going so fast it passed Schmidt by. It took half an hour to turn the liner around and maneuver it into position to pick him up. Officers dropped a handful of life preservers in the water, climbed down a rope ladder and stretched out their arms to help Schmidt aboard. Remarkably, after a bath and a hot cup of coffee, he was well enough to join other survivors on deck. Schmidt survived the ordeal with both his life and his life savings intact. Underneath the gray cap he wore were six soggy five hundred dollar bills.

The rescue of Carl Schmidt as photographed by a *Berlin* passenger. (*Wide World*)

LAST DANCE OF THE VESTRIS

With Schmidt safely aboard, Captain von Thulen decided to conclude his rescue mission. He radioed his ship's progress: "After rescuing twenty-two persons out of No. 13, we picked up Carl Schmidt, who had been drifting in a life belt for twenty-two hours. All safe and sound. Nobody injured. Lots of small wreckage drifting. Very strong northerly winds. Squally and high seas. Arrive Ambrose Light Wednesday, 4 a.m." Reporters already writing about the stamina of the Pluckiest Pair had yet another hero—Schmidt became the disaster's Iron Man.

At 3:00 p.m., Admiral Taylor sent a wireless message to the Navy Department to let them know the airship *U.S.S. Los Angeles* wouldn't be needed. The Lakehurst, New Jersey-based Zeppelin had been placed on alert to deploy to the disaster scene to search for survivors from the air. An hour later, Taylor radioed again, this time to offer his own assessment of the rescue operation's future: "Use of destroyers not recommended. Rough sea, wind about forty five miles per hour. As all lifeboats are accounted for, consider search beyond nightfall today useless." Even so, the *Wyoming* would remain on scene. Instead of allowing the battleship to return home, Taylor's superiors ordered him to stay and continue searching.

Meanwhile, the dreadnought's crew did the best they could to make their harvest of the sea as comfortable as possible. The ship's tailor took the female survivors' measurements to make skirts for them out of sailors' white dress uniforms. Navy blue jumpers were supplied for blouses and hat ribbons for headbands. When it was revealed the ladies needed hairpins, sailors improvised them out of pieces of wire and gave them as gifts.

As it turned out, the *Wyoming* didn't find anyone else alive on the waves, making Schmidt the last and perhaps the luckiest of the *Vestris* victims to be rescued. Sadly, if there were still others adrift in life belts, they didn't have long before their nightmares mercifully came to an end. Whether it was due to luck, skill or a combination of both, Cumings, von Thulen, Forey and Overstreet succeeded where other captains did not. The *Ohio Maru, San Juan* and the Grace liner *Santa*

"TAKE HOLD OF ONE END, AND I'LL TAKE THE OTHER"

Barbara spent hours searching, but were unable to find anyone living or dead. The *Santa Barbara's* skipper couldn't be blamed—his vessel had part of its bridge ripped away by the same storm that sank the *Vestris*.

The next morning, the *Wyoming's* Roman Catholic chaplain said a requiem Mass at the wreck scene before the battleship turned for Norfolk. With the primary rescue vessels steaming home, the work of locating anyone still in the water fell to the destroyers *Davis* and *Shaw*, and four Coast Guard cutters. It had now been more than forty-eight hours since the *Vestris* was swallowed by the sea and naval officers believed it was doubtful any swimmers were still alive. The Gulf Stream water was warm, but there was no question the elements were too extreme for even the most robust castaway to endure. No one could withstand the pummeling the stormy sea continued to dish out, nor the chilly air that blanketed the ocean after sunset. Accordingly, the destroyers' mission would be one of recovery. Officers determined life belts would keep the dead afloat for several days and the current would scatter them over a wide area. They had their work cut out for them.

Stokers Joseph Boxill, John Morris and Gerald Burton aboard the *Wyoming*. (*International Newsreel*)

Throughout the rest of the day, the government ships continued searching despite the squally and ever-worsening weather. Even so, the men of the *Shaw* still managed to recover the remains of First Class passenger Karl Franke, his daughter Ingeborg, Major Inouye and an unidentified man. The *Davis* recovered nine bodies and transferred them to the *Shaw*, where they were wrapped in canvas and respectfully laid out on deck. Many had been badly mutilated by sharks. The body of one man was in such awful condition there was no way he could be identified. The *Shaw's* crew buried him at sea. As night fell, a storm blew in that rivaled the one that sent the *Vestris* to the bottom. The little ships endured such severe punishment at the hands of the wind and waves they were forced to call off their searches and return to base.

The cutter *Manning* transmitted a summary of her activities. The description of one tiny body brought the sinking's impact home in a particularly graphic and chilling manner: "One Negro child, name unknown, aged six or seven, height 3 feet 11 inches, weight 40 pounds, blue dress, lavender waist, gray coat, tan shoes and stockings, imitation pearl necklace." It was 5-year-old Mildred Headley. She died along with her mother, father and two sisters.

While en route to New York, the technology that was used to save the lives of *Vestris* passengers and crew became employed in the effort to tell their stories to a public hungry for news of the disaster. The *Shipper's* wireless room came alive with inquiries from news organizations looking for a scoop. Cumings and others were solicited for their accounts and, on the off chance any were taken, their photographs: "Commander American Shipper. We will greatly appreciate short wireless report of your gallant rescue with names of passengers rescued—The New York Times." And to the *Shipper's* "official photographer" from the Associated Press: "Please purchase rescue pictures for us. Will pay liberally will meet you at destination."

In addition to the race for news, the race to obstruct justice had begun. Reunited on the *American Shipper*, Johnson and Welland began planning for the firestorm that was undoubtedly headed their way when they reached landfall. The men were frantic about the *Vestris's* draft and how the fact she was overloaded would be received by the public. Worse than that, they feared what investigators would have to say about it. It was in the midst of one of their discussions that Captain Cumings entered the room and offered the men advice. "I don't want

"TAKE HOLD OF ONE END, AND I'LL TAKE THE OTHER"

to hear anything about the disaster," he said. "But be loyal to your company."

The *Vestris* officers agreed with Cumings and came to the conclusion the most important thing they could do was get back to England without broaching the topic of the draft in the United States. After all, the U.S. had no law on the books when it came to load lines, so it was possible no one would even ask. They agreed to do whatever was necessary to keep the whole overloading business out of the expected inquiries.

Captain Schuyler Forbes Cumings. (*Underwood & Underwood*)

While Johnson and Welland schemed, Cumings received from his wife what had to have been the most gratifying wireless message of the entire operation: "Congratulations so proud love. Mary."

CHAPTER FIFTEEN

"Thank God You Are Safe"

Wireless messages exchanged between the four rescue vessels enabled Cumings to calculate the human toll of the disaster. The numbers related a heartbreaking story. Most of the *Vestris's* 128 passengers remained unaccounted for. The crew fared a bit better, but dozens were still missing. Cumings scribbled the numbers on a blank wireless slip.

Meanwhile, employees at Lamport and Holt's Manhattan offices put all other duties aside in an effort to obtain as much information as possible for the worried friends and family of *Vestris* passengers and crew. E. George Williams and his staff found themselves inundated with hundreds of telegrams and phone calls. As passenger traffic manager for the firm of Sanderson and Son, Lamport and Holt's New York business agents, Williams answered each inquiry as quickly as he could. Unfortunately, details were slow in coming and updates were incomplete, at best. If that wasn't enough, Williams was also tasked with answering the seemingly endless questions shouted by reporters: "What news?"

"Are they saved?"

"Where are the lists?"

"We know some boats have been picked up," he told the crowd packed into his lobby. "But we have only the names of those on the French oil tanker *Myriam*. As soon as we learn something definite we'll notify you." Heartbroken relatives turned away in grief, but Williams offered them what would sadly turn out to be false hope. He communicated the company's belief some survivors had been picked up by a vessel which lacked a radio and the number of missing was expected to drop dramatically as soon as all ships were accounted for. Williams was only partly right.

Williams received several inquiries from the friends and family of William Adams. The businessman contacted his family from the *American Shipper*, but his name hadn't yet made it onto the lists of those saved. Williams determined he survived when telegrams addressed to Adams began to trickle into the office. A message from Adams's wife read simply: "Thank God you are safe."

Nevertheless, for every scrap of good news there was gut-wrenching sorrow. A desperate message from Mexico City came in inquiring as to the fate of the Franke family. The sender would find out soon enough that Mr. and Mrs. Carlos Franke, their son Helmuth and daughter Ingeborg were all dead, one of five families wiped out when the *Vestris* went down. A relative of First Class passenger Isaac Nahen was calling every ten minutes. The man would eventually learn the father of eight was dead. A relative of 27-year-old First Class passenger Agnes Johnson was cheered by the news Agnes's brother Campbell Kellman had been saved, but the young woman's name would eventually appear on the list of the drowned.

Only sixty of the 128 passengers who embarked the ship at Hoboken were picked up by rescue ships. Twenty-eight of thirty-six women and all thirteen children were lost. In addition, forty-five of the 197 crew were drowned. In all, 115 people were presumed dead including the entire Jackson family, the Brownfields, Keith Burt, Gladys Stevens, Sidney Koppe, Earl Devore, Charlotte and Lisolette Puppe, Vincenzo Murri, Chief Steward Davies, Laundress Margaret McCulloch and scores of others.

Captain W.W. Pugh, master of the Lamport and Holt liner *Swinburne*, was among the crowd in the lobby. Pugh was there to find out if his brother, *Vestris* Purser Albert Pugh had survived, but he was told there was no news of his whereabouts. After reviewing the lists without seeing his brother's name, Captain Pugh left the office and began to cry. Five minutes later, a revised list from the *American Shipper* came in that included Albert Pugh's name among the saved. A telephone call was quickly placed to alert the grief-stricken family that Albert was alive.

PASSENGERS SAVED AND DROWNED

	Men Aboard	Men Saved	Women Aboard	Women Saved	Children Aboard	Children Saved
First Class	41	28	15	4	6	0
Second Class	12	9	8	1	0	N/A
Third Class	26	15	13	3	7	0
Total	79	52	36	8	13	0

Note: The table excludes two deportees, one male and one female, both of whom were lost.

When it came to the human toll of accidents involving British shipping, Liverpool was always hard-hit due to the overwhelming number of crew members who made their homes there. In the *Vestris's* case, the city was home to her captain, officers and the great majority of her stewards and engineers. Consequently, Lamport and Holt's Liverpool offices were besieged by the wives of crewmen waiting for news of their husbands. Some of them had no choice but to take their babies along for the excruciating vigil.

Vestris Assistant Purser Leslie Jones had just arrived in England for two months leave when he heard of the loss of his ship. He had been at sea aboard the *Celtic* when the *Vestris* sank and wasn't immediately informed of the disaster. He also went to the office to await news. "The ordeal of not knowing what has happened to my pals is terrible," he told a reporter. "I pray to God they may be saved." Jones went on to praise Carey and the ship itself. "I have been in her for two years and during that time have made many voyages between New York and Buenos Aires," he said. "I loved the *Vestris*, and words fail me to describe my sorrow that I shall see her no more."

RESCUE SHIP TOTALS

	Passengers	Crew
American Shipper	41	84
Myriam	9	47
Berlin	5	18
Wyoming	5	3
Total	60	152

Captain Carey's sons and daughters gathered at the family home in the Liverpool suburb of Great Crosby to await updates with their mother. Reporters were there, too. "I am a little worried, naturally," Carey's son Matthew said. "The family have confidence in him; in fact, my mother told me that she only expected to be awakened if any definite news came through. She was a little anxious last night but quite hopeful." Mrs. Carey's agony turned to joy when her husband was reported saved. The story was carried by British newspapers beneath the headline *"Vestris Captain Safe."* It claimed "the master of the *Vestris*" was among those rescued by the *Berlin*. Some jubilant family members left the house to tell neighbors the good news, but their sense of relief didn't last long. The Careys went into mourning when the truth was learned. Newsmen hit the streets of Liverpool with renewed vigor in search of any tidbit about the late captain's life. An Associated Press reporter located the taxi driver who took Carey to the docks a couple of weeks before. "He was a fine figure of a man," the cabbie said of the tragic captain. "And he was very jovial when he went away from home here."

While en route to New York, *Berlin* passengers created a fund for the crewmen of lifeboat No. 13 and the collection raised just over five hundred dollars. Around 8:30 a.m. Wednesday, the ship became the first rescue vessel to arrive in New York Harbor. The *Berlin* was guided to her pier by a handful of tugs, followed by a small flotilla of boats carrying reporters and newsreel cameramen.

After having been notified by Lamport and Holt the night before that his wife, *Vestris* Stewardess Laurinda Moore had been picked up by the *Berlin*, Edwin Moore traveled from his home in Jersey City to reunite with her. He and Laurinda's son, William Syphers, joined the multitude on the pier waiting for the ship to arrive. A reporter observed that of the five hundred, there were only "a mere handful of relatives and friends." The rest were curious locals eager to get a glimpse of the rescue ship itself. As the *Berlin* came in, Moore and Syphers scanned the rail impatiently, but they couldn't pick Laurinda out of the crowd.

After the gangway was put in place, the *Berlin's* regular passengers were disembarked first. Next, the weary *Vestris* passengers and crew began coming ashore one by one. Moore was not among them. Long after the last survivor had departed the pier, the two men were still there—looking for any trace of their loved one.

While Moore and Syphers searched, a reporter chatted with a very proud Carl Schmidt. "Say, look at me," the survivor said as he thumped his chest. "I'm a big, strong man. I'm forty-five years old and I haven't even caught a cold. I can handle anything." The Iron Man showed the reporter his black-and-blue shoulders. "These are welcome wounds," he said.

About an hour later, the *American Shipper* made her appearance. The vessel presented a highly unusual sight as she tied up at the American Merchant Lines pier—her decks packed with people who looked completely out of place aboard a liner completing a transatlantic crossing. As they did for the *Berlin*, newsreel cameras rolled to document the ship's arrival and to obtain precious shots of stunned survivors. Many former *Vestris* passengers were still wearing the first things they were able to throw on when they heard the rumor to abandon ship. Others wore a hodge-podge of clothing given them by *Shipper* passengers. Nearly all the men were unshaven and survivors of both sexes were without shoes. One reporter described them as appearing more bewildered than distressed.

The *Vestris* crew looked even worse, but the great majority managed to remain cheerful despite their situation. Sailors and stewards huddled on deck smiling, waving, smoking and even cheering for the cameramen. Most were still haggard and filthy. Some were wrapped in blankets, while others wore trousers and coats either too big or too small. Many were barefoot and had wrapped strips of cloth around their feet in an effort to keep warm. One blanket-wearing sailor was completely naked underneath; another held a striped tom cat. Steward Alfred Dineley escaped the *Vestris* with ship's mascot, Tiger Lil. Dineley held the tabby close, as he did throughout the stormy night in the lifeboat.

Only a few hundred people, including about a dozen newspapermen, came out to greet the *American Shipper*. Although press coverage of the *Vestris* sinking was intense, the tens of thousands who gathered to see the *Carpathia* in 1912 stayed home this time. Pauline Royal, wife of *Vestris* Saxophonist Ray Royal, waited in the crowd with a friend. It had been an excruciating couple of days for her, as Ray was first reported missing then saved. She was so overcome she could barely speak. Catherine Johnson and her 7-year-old son waited for Edward Johnson. The wife and four sisters of Edward Marvin were there to greet him. Family and friends also waited for Herman Rueckert and First Class passenger Ernesto Permuy. The two women there for Permuy were from Columbia and couldn't read English. When they arrived at the pier, someone read his name to them from a list of survivors. They were greatly relieved to hear it.

Jubilant *Vestris* survivors aboard the *Berlin*. From left to right: Third Class passenger Henry Schultz, Steward Thomas Evans, Steward Albert Knill, Steward Thomas Boyd, Second Steward Duncan, Deck Steward Percy Hudson and Third Engineer Harry Forsyth. (*Wide World*)

The crowd surged toward the *American Shipper* when the gangway was moved into position. A dozen police officers from the Greenwich Street station struggled to hold people back while survivors disembarked. The bruised and battered *Vestris* passengers came down first—many of them limping toward land. Shouts of joy were heard as families reunited. Ray Royal was still wearing his bandsman's uniform when he jumped into the arms of his wife. The couple hugged for many minutes. Right behind Royal was Band Leader Andrew Bartozzi, who was met by his mother. A pair of somber representatives of the Mormon Church greeted David Huish.

Members of the *Vestris* crew were easy to pick out. Stewards and waiters still wore their white jackets. Engineers came down in overalls. Edwin Moore and William Syphers, who first believed Stewardess Laurinda Moore to be on the *Berlin*, met her as she came ashore sobbing inconsolably. "Oh those babies, those children," she wailed. "To think they, so young, had to lose their lives while we old folks were saved." A visibly shaken Purser Pugh turned away when a reporter questioned him about the wreck. "I never want to open my lips about it as long as I live," he said.

S.S. Berlin arrives in New York Harbor. (*International Newsreel*)

Despite the smaller crowd, comparisons to the *Carpathia's* dramatic arrival of sixteen years before were undeniable and it wasn't long before Captain Cumings discovered he was among the most celebrated heroes of the disaster. Cumings mugged for newsreel cameras just outside the *American Shipper's* bridge, but he soon expressed frustration with reporters' endless questions. "I've done my job," he told them. "Now won't you leave me alone?"

In addition to winning approval from an admiring public, his bosses were pleased with his work. *The New York Times* reported, "Shipping Board officials likened the achievement of the *American Shipper* to the feat of Captain Rostron of the *Carpathia* in rescuing survivors of the *Titanic*," and declared it "One of the most brilliant achievements in the annals of the American Merchant Marine."

A newsreel cameraman found Lionel Licorish sitting atop one of the *Shipper's* lifeboats. The few seconds of film he shot showed Licorish staring into the camera and taking off his cap to give moviegoers a better view of his boyish face. Anne Devore's image was captured by the same camera crew, sitting on a hatch cover holding Speedway Lady. Stewards Alfred Dineley and James Rae were photographed with Tiger Lil. Within hours, the wire services would transmit the photos around the world for publication. The *Chicago Tribune* ran the accounts of Devore and Dineley under the headline, "*Owners Refuse To Desert Pets When Quitting Sinking Ship.*" Some readers were moved to send Devore hate mail, attacking her for saving her dog's life while her husband was left to drown.

Anne Devore and Speedway Lady. (*Wide World*)

"THANK GOD YOU ARE SAFE"

Martin McEvilly stood in the crowd waiting for Fred Hanson to come ashore. The veteran *New York Daily News* photographer was a daredevil in his own right, having made his mark a few years before when he shot photos from a circling airplane of the U.S. Navy's attempt to salvage a wrecked submarine. This assignment would prove to be much easier. Editors found out about Hanson's photographs from a wireless message sent from the *Shipper* by William Wills Davies, Hanson's boat mate in lifeboat No. 1. McEvilly's mission was to make a deal with Hanson, retrieve the film and get it back to the *Daily News* as quickly as possible.

Hanson came down the gangway and was greeted by McEvilly. The men shook hands and stepped away from the crowd where they could discuss matters privately. McEvilly offered to buy the film, but the shy Hanson had no idea what it was worth. After some discussion they reached an agreement. The newspaper would develop the film and if the photos were usable, Hanson would be paid an amount he believed to be "generous." McEvilly made his way back to the newsroom with the pantryman, the film and the scoop.

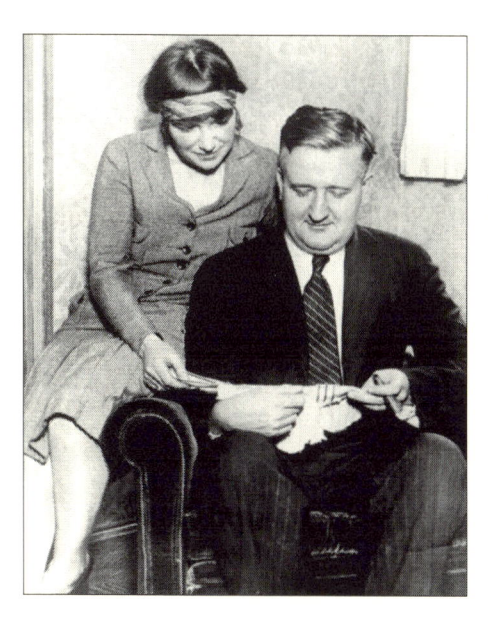

Edward Marvin shows his wife the piece of life belt he saved as a souvenir. (*Associated Press*)

LAST DANCE OF THE VESTRIS

While happy reunions took place around him, an increasingly desperate Edward Henrotin searched for his brother. 50-year-old mining engineer Charles Henrotin had been traveling First Class on the *Vestris* and was not listed among the rescued. Edward was hoping against hope the lists were wrong. He worked the crowd, going from survivor to survivor asking if they had any information about his brother, but his face steeled as more and more survivors came off the ship without news of Charles. Henrotin began to fear he had seen his brother for the last time; his questions became more frantic when the crowd started thinning out. When all the survivors had departed the pier, Edward Henrotin stayed near the ship in the hopes he could find some scrap of hope. He didn't. His brother Charles was dead.

Steward James Rae and Tiger Lil. (*Wide World*)

The most seriously-injured crew members were helped off the ship and taken by ambulance to Long Island College Hospital. Passengers were driven to hotels or transported home at Lamport and Holt's expense. Officers went to the Hotel Holley at Washington Square, while the scores of other crewmen were taken by bus to the much less luxurious Seamen's Church Institute. Two Red Cross nurses and a representative of the Travelers Aid Society were on the pier to offer assistance, but just in case, Father John Grogan of Our Lady of the Rosary Church was also there to offer the use of his rectory to anyone without a place to stay.

To avoid the bureaucratic hassle that went along with entering New York Harbor in an official capacity, the *Myriam* stopped near Coney Island around 11:30 p.m. Wednesday and transferred her load of survivors to the tugboat that would take them the rest of the way. As the *William F. Dalzell* chugged ahead, the brightly lit Brooklyn Bridge sent exhausted survivors the very powerful message they were almost home. The tugboat steamed under the bridge and docked at Pier 8, in Brooklyn. The *Myriam's* load of survivors were greeted by loved ones, reporters, photographers and curious members of the public.

Wilma Slaughter was one of the first off the tug, looking fetching in her French sailor's uniform. Her husband had come in on the *American Shipper* and was waiting for her. The two ran to one another and embraced passionately. It was like a scene out of a talkie. The couple was besieged by newsmen. "The captain did his duty," Slaughter told them. Then she cut the interview short. "Now, I want to get some sleep because I have to get up early to buy some new clothes," she said. With that, Cline Slaughter whisked his wife away to a waiting car and a restful night at Manhattan's posh Commodore Hotel.

Lamport and Holt officials were on the pier to pick up Second Officer Watson, who was also being pressed by reporters. An executive shooed the newsmen away, "Leave him alone. He's all in." The company also had busses and a handful of cars waiting to take the dozens of stewards and stokers to the Seamen's Church Institute. Upon arrival, each crewman was assigned a bed, issued meal vouchers and given ten dollars spending money.

The next day, the *Wyoming* steamed into Norfolk carrying Batten and the others. The survivors didn't have much to say to the reporters who managed to climb onto the battleship as it docked. They were transferred to a hospital barge and taken to Portsmouth Naval Hospital to be checked out. Newsmen were waiting for them when they arrived. At least one enterprising reporter was able to ask Marion Batten a few questions before she went off to bed. She told him how her group survived. "If it hadn't been for Gerald, we wouldn't be here," she said in reference to Stoker Burton. Mary Ulrich's husband, Otto, who was picked up by the *American Shipper,* came down from New York to greet his wife. The couple was reunited at the hospital. All but Teruko Inouye were discharged the next day, whereupon they boarded northbound trains. Inouye would remain an extra night before heading to New York City for her husband's funeral.

Coast Guard cutters *Tucker* and *Acushnet* were the first recovery ships to arrive in New York after experiencing some success recovering corpses in the heavy seas. The *Acushnet* carried the lifeless body of the man who mixed Dana and Sorensen their drinks just seventy-two hours before, 39-year-old Bartender Thomas Jones. Also on board were the remains of 28-year-old First Class passenger Ralph Whitehead and Third Class passengers Ramon Garcia Pelal and Jose Gonzalez Rua. Along with nearly eight thousand dollars in cash and checks tucked into Rua's life belt, sailors found a pair of toddler's shoes. The body of their owner, 2-year-old Jorge Rua, was never found. The last of the recovery ships to limp in was the storm-battered *Shaw.* Admiral Taylor turned out to be right when he advised the navy to recall its destroyers. The *Shaw* had been seriously damaged by the storm.

An official from the Japanese consulate was waiting to claim Major Inouye's body when the destroyer tied up at the pier. All other remains were transferred to Sea View Morgue in Staten Island, where more than a hundred grieving relatives visited in an attempt to identify loved ones. In addition, some of the sailors lounging around the Seamen's Church Institute were sent to ID shipmates. Hero Fifth Engineer John Jones was identified thanks to the signet ring he wore. The body of Steward Frank Rigg still wore a white jacket. An official from Ellis Island identified the remains of deportee Sarah Leacock. The final *Vestris* body to be claimed was that of 42-year-old Third Class passenger Nora Kanan of Detroit. A relative recognized her tattoos—a fish on the back of each of her hands.

Within a couple of weeks, the thrilling moving pictures shot aboard the rescue ships had been distributed worldwide and, on one occasion, created headlines of their own. While watching a newsreel at a movie theater in Glasgow, the sister of *Vestris* Steward John Ross was shocked to see the image of a man who looked remarkably like her long-lost brother. Ross left Scotland years before and lost touch with his family. His sister wanted to make sure it was him she saw on the big screen, so after the movie was over she made her way to the offices of the British Gaumont Company. She watched the film again and confirmed her eyes had not deceived her. John Ross had survived the sinking of the *Vestris*.

CHAPTER SIXTEEN

"They Were Murderers"

The first news stories about the *Vestris* disaster were written from intercepted wireless messages. The information they contained was incomplete at best and at its worst, wildly inaccurate. Reporters had to wait for survivors to come ashore to hear their accounts firsthand to finally get the facts straight. Stories containing dockside interviews hit newsstands printed beneath such headlines as, *"Boats Sink with Women and Children"* and *"Deaths Held to SOS Delay."* The *Baltimore News* screamed *"Crew of Vestris Took Best Boats."*

"Blame Captain for Sea Tragedy," trumpeted the *Omaha Bee-News,* while the *New York Herald Tribune* ran the grisly, *"Babies Crushed to Death."*

At the *Daily News,* Fred Hanson's freshly developed photographs were rushed to the desk of publisher Joseph Medill Patterson. With just one look, Patterson knew he'd struck gold. Hanson's photographs were all very good, but two were extraordinary. Patterson ordered them printed immediately. The publisher also doubled the price Hanson was asking. As copies flew off newsstands, the generous and grateful

Patterson doubled the payment yet again. The final amount was rumored to have been in the neighborhood of $5,000, and in a year where the average worker's annual salary was just under $1,500, it wasn't a bad payday for the castaway shutterbug.

Fred Hanson took his famous photographs with an eight dollar and fifty cent Eastman Kodak Hawk-Eye folding camera. (*Sheila Rosamond*)

Hanson's visuals told a thrilling story by themselves, but they appeared with articles containing gruesome descriptions of the sinking and a slew of inflammatory accusations. Grieving survivors furious at having lost loved ones were all too happy to share every detail about the leaky old liner and its incompetent crew. A livid Captain Sorensen took the lead. "I know all about ships," he told a *Chicago Daily Tribune* reporter. "And I can say that the reason the *Vestris* foundered is due to criminal neglect." He was only getting warmed up. "And as for the members of the crew who refused to pick up women on a foundering lifeboat, leaving them to drown; they were murderers," Sorensen said. The veteran seafarer and nearly everyone else laid the lion's share of blame for the disaster squarely at the feet of Captain Carey. Officially, Orrin Stevens's bride of three months was missing, but he knew she probably lost her life when the lifeboat she was in was smashed to bits by the falling beam. Stevens picked up where Sorensen left off. "It was criminal negligence," he said. "The officers were all murderers. They were brave enough, but they had no brains."

The accusation became a common refrain. "The women and children in the boats were murdered as plainly as if they had been hit over the head with a hatchet," former First Class passenger T.E. Mack said. "If Captain Carey and his crew had carefully looked after the details of saving the lives of those on board the ship, everybody would be alive today. The captain and most of his men acted like a bunch of old farmers."

"No one told us what to do," Fred Puppe complained. "And no one seemed to care." Herman Rueckert spoke to the exemplary behavior of the passengers. "What panic there was, was confined to the crew," he said. However, it was the enigmatic Ovelton Maxey who really had Carey's number. "It seems obvious that the Captain was stalling for time in the hope of saving his ship for salvage purposes," Maxey said. "He put the financial considerations of his company above those of his passengers and his crew. He delayed sending an SOS just to save a few dollars." Maxey also joined in the chorus of survivors accusing the captain of murder "quite as much as if he had held a pistol at the head of his human charges."

The *Times* reported the harsh criticism was "almost unanimous" among survivors:

> They accused the company of failure to provide adequate safety equipment, the ship's master of inefficiency and vacillation in the face of danger, his officers of callous indifference and the crew as a whole with downright cowardice, panic, desertion and brutal neglect of passengers.

Even some members of the ship's crew joined in. Musician Ray Royal called the evacuation "most inefficient," while Steward Samuel Sadowski blamed the ship itself, asserting, "Every porthole was defective." Former *Vestris* Steward Alfred Mooney found his way into the news by missing the boat. Mooney told a *Baltimore Sun* reporter the ship was so unseaworthy, he quit before her final voyage. "When I got back to New York I was too scared to sail on her again and I didn't," he said. "That was the luckiest decision I ever made."

The general opinion of the British press was that the coverage produced by their counterparts across the Pond was entirely too salacious. The *Manchester Guardian* was especially vocal in its disgust, openly referring to the American press as "yellow." The paper accused the *New York Herald Tribune* of reporting conjecture as fact in an article in which Captain Carey's emotional state was analyzed. The *Tribune* interviewed a handful of psychologists who blamed Carey's breakdown on "mental paralysis." The experts were of the opinion Carey originally underestimated the peril the *Vestris* was in, and as the situation worsened, became so horrified by developments he simply couldn't act. "There can be no question," the article concluded, "of Captain Carey's courage or his desire to do the right thing, but it seems the ocean floor, like hell, is paved with good intentions."

The stories were contributing to what had become an epic public relations disaster for Lamport and Holt with no end in sight. In an early and weak attempt at damage control, Sanderson and Sons Vice President David Cook cited the results of the recent once-over by the Steamboat Inspection Service that certified the ship and her lifeboats as seaworthy. Cook also praised Carey, calling him "One of our best captains." However, it was Colonel Samuel Heywood Melly, a Liverpool-based Lamport and Holt manager, who went the farthest. "We wish to give absolute denial to the assertion that the crew of the *Vestris* was inexperienced and we feel there can be no doubt that the boats were lowered at the right time," he said. "We have every confidence in Captain Carey and his crew."

LAST DANCE OF THE VESTRIS

The company received some much needed help when a handful of crewmen came forward to defend Carey. Second Steward Duncan penned an open letter to the British Embassy to clear the air about Carey's mental state while the *Vestris* was going down. He wrote:

> Captain Carey had all his faculties until the last. He oversaw everything and gave orders who was to go into each boat and how to lower it. He never left the boat deck and was cool and collected until he went down with his vessel. To my mind he did everything that was proper and possible to save his passengers and ship.

Carey's half-brother traveled nearly 2,400 miles from Calgary to New York City to represent the family while the late captain's affairs were sorted out. "I do not feel that the public can justify pile-up slander against my departed half-brother on account of the recent tragedy," Arthur Heffernan said. "I knew him as well as anybody in the world and can conscientiously say that he was a brave and cautious seaman." Sir Burton Chadwick of the Honorable Company of Master Mariners joined in to protest what he called the "wild and cruel injustice" being done to Carey and to ask that judgment be withheld pending an official investigation.

Sir Burton's wish came true. In an effort to determine what happened to the *Vestris*, two inquiries were initiated. The first would be led by Charles H. Tuttle, U.S. Attorney for the Southern District of New York. Tuttle explained why the United States was right to take the lead when it came to questions of jurisdiction:

> The *Vestris* sailed from this port and the survivors are being brought here. I am informed the ship's papers were documented in this port. Under the circumstances this office will proceed at once before United States Commissioner Francis A. O'Neill to gather and perpetuate the facts.

Tuttle wanted to hear from as many witnesses as possible before they left the city, so his staff issued dozens of Doe subpoenas to survivors as they came off the rescue ships. A notice was also placed in newspapers urging any who were missed at the piers to assemble at Lower Manhattan's City Hall Post Office and Courthouse beginning at 10:30 a.m. Thursday.

Charles Tuttle was still relatively new to his assignment, having been appointed by President Coolidge the year before. For his part, Commissioner O'Neill spent most of his time hearing cases related to Prohibition, though he secretly believed the Volstead Act to be unenforceable. The Republican had twice run for elective office unsuccessfully, but among his greatest accomplishments was a fight he won. The 51-year-old fought at the Battle of San Juan Hill during the Spanish American War. Tuttle and O'Neill were ambitious men, but neither was an authority on maritime law, a fact that would complicate matters as their investigation plodded ahead.

The U.S. Steamboat Inspection Service initiated the other inquiry at the Customs House. Its purpose was to determine whether Edward Keane and his team of inspectors were negligent when they cleared the *Vestris* to go to sea. If the men were found at fault, the evidence would be turned over to the U.S. Attorney for possible criminal charges. The investigation was headed by Assistant Commerce Secretary Walter Folger Brown and Dickerson N. Hoover, Supervising Inspector General of the Steamboat Inspection Service and brother of F.B.I. Director J. Edgar Hoover.

Of all potential witnesses, the surviving officers were the most critical to understanding how the disaster unfolded, but securing their presence at the inquiries was turning out to be a challenge. Johnson and Welland were holed-up in the Hotel Holley with Sanderson and Son executives and a pair of lawyers from the Manhattan law firm of Burlingham, Veeder, Masten and Fearey. On the evening the men arrived on board the *American Shipper*, a deputy U.S. Marshal went to the hotel to serve Johnson and Welland with a subpoena, but left without seeing them. A reporter from the *Herald Tribune* asked where they were. "The men are very tired and are resting," David Cook said. "It would be cruel to disturb them." There was some truth to the statement, but their fatigue may have had something to do with the intense preparation for their testimonies and not necessarily from their exertions in the Gulf Stream. It ended up taking marshals two days to catch up with the chief officer. Second Officer Watson's excuse was legitimate. He was still in the hospital.

Lamport and Holt's retention of the high-powered law firm was evidence of the company's intention to fight the *Vestris* firestorm with fire. Lead partner Charles Culp Burlingham was among the foremost authorities on Admiralty Law in the country. He famously defended the White Star Line before the Supreme Court following the *Titanic* disaster and won a victory limiting the company's liability to just $91,000 when the victims' relatives had been seeking thirteen million. Under very similar circumstances, Burlingham did his job in 1912 and he was well-prepared to do it again.

In an effort to get the officers back to England without broaching the subject of overloading, it was decided to coach them to give the "correct" answers if and when draft-related questions were raised. The sessions didn't go smoothly. As the officers sat in their hotel room recounting the sinking as they remembered it, they were frequently interrupted by attorneys who urged them to "Put it some other way," or "Do not bother saying that." Both men were skeptical of the lawyers' motives. Johnson didn't trust them and consequently didn't offer much information. The frayed chief officer became so stressed out he had to consult a doctor for help with his nerves.

The coaching intensified when Lamport and Holt Assistant Marine Superintendent William Heasley showed up at the hotel. Heasley wanted to make sure everyone was on the same page. "What draft have you got?" He asked Johnson.

"Twenty-six feet six inches and twenty-seven feet eleven inches."

"Good God no!" Heasley snapped.

"What have you got?" Johnson asked.

"Twenty-six feet two inches and twenty-seven feet three inches." Faced with the certain end of his career if he did not obey, the chief officer gave in, "That is good enough for me, then."

"THEY WERE MURDERERS"

Heasley dealt with Watson next. They met at the law office following the second officer's release from the hospital. Watson's recollection of the draft was also "incorrect," so Heasley produced a sheet of paper with his own figures written on it and laid it on a table. He pointed to it and looked at Watson. "This is the draft we are using."

"All right," Watson answered glumly. After what the second officer had just been through, he would have agreed to anything.

Dubbed the Tuttle Inquiry by newspapers, the proceeding began on the afternoon of Thursday, November 15. There were unforeseen complications before it even began. So many people had packed into O'Neill's courtroom the investigation had to be moved to a larger auditorium at the last minute. Outside, Tuttle announced his objectives to the assembled reporters. The truth would be learned, he said, and if anyone was found criminally responsible, that person or persons would be arrested pending indictments from the grand jury.

On the first day of testimony, Puppe, Rueckert, Quiros and a handful of others testified to the disorganization of the crew and the shoddy condition of the lifeboats. Quiros said the Barbadians in the boat that picked him up were armed with truncheons, and he raised eyebrows when he related the story of how a stoker was threatened on deck. "One officer tried to shoot a Negro, who grabbed the gun and threw it overboard," he said. It was the only time Quiros would mention the incident in any of his accounts. If it ever occurred, other witnesses either died in the sinking or chose to remain silent. No other survivor would ever speak of it.

It was inevitable the issue of race would find its way into both the news coverage and court proceedings. A handful of white crewmen began finger-pointing at their black counterparts, blaming them for a host of misdeeds. Despite the heroism of Lionel Licorish, Gerald Burton, Joseph Boxill and others, the *Vestris's* Barbadian crew members were vilified when the story of the firemen's abandonment of the stokehold became known. Under the headline, "*Panic of Negro Firemen Blamed for Disaster,*" the *Guardian* published a Reuter's story wherein a handful of engineers "attributed the disaster to the action of panic-stricken Negro firemen in refusing to stay down below." Hundreds of papers also carried the account of Marion Batten's having been pushed by a black crewman, and Anne Devore's comments about the callousness of some of the Barbadians in lifeboat No. 1 didn't help matters.

Even Lionel Licorish was attacked for his conduct immediately following the sinking. Second Refrigerating Engineer Ernest Smith told anyone who would listen that he, and not the hero quartermaster had been in charge of lifeboat No. 14. Smith claimed he had already taken command by the time Licorish swam up and that Licorish obeyed his orders once he was in the boat. Sorensen stepped forward to defend Licorish and Smith's protestations never amounted to anything.

From the Seamen's Church Institute, Fireman Samuel Parfitt reacted to the criticism by telling a *Times* reporter "not a white man would have been saved" had it not been for the below decks efforts of his countrymen. Black crew members had other supporters, as well. Edward Walcott, who was fished out of the water by lifeboat No. 3, praised the boat's Barbadian crew, saying, "There were four colored men aboard who behaved better than the white men."

One social justice group had heard enough. The American Negro Labor Congress held a meeting in Harlem to lambaste the press and both inquiries, accusing them of trying to whitewash the actions of white officers and crew while unfairly blaming the sinking on black crew members. Some newspapers agreed and joined in their defense. The *Hartford Currant* wrote:

> One cannot load all the responsibility on the West Indians who were supposed to be in the boiler room. They were not trained seals nor did they have wings at that time, and it was apparently necessary to swim or fly in order to get about.

Of the dozens of survivors who testified at the inquiries, it turned out to be Sorensen who had the most difficult time getting his story straight. During his testimony at the Hoover inquiry, Sorensen backed away from statements he gave reporters upon his arrival aboard the

American Shipper. On the stand, the mariner said newsmen "twisted and sometimes made exactly opposite" his words when they reported his claims that the men of the *Vestris* were cowards and the ship's lifeboats rotten. In a major about-face, Sorensen told investigators the boats were in "first class" condition.

Later that evening, Sorensen took to the airwaves to set the record straight in the court of public opinion. He told WLTH radio he had been "shamefully misquoted" by reporters. Sorensen's remarks were a far cry from the ire he directed at all things Lamport and Holt just a day before:

> In my opinion Captain Carey was a brave man. When he saw the ship was doomed he followed the old traditions of the sea and went down with his ship. I think anybody with a heart would forgive a man's mistake, which he willingly paid for with his own life. The majority of the officers and crew in my opinion were brave and true seamen and did wonderfully well under difficult circumstances.

Meanwhile, there wasn't a lot for *Vestris* crewmen to do at the Seamen's Church Institute while they waited for the inquiries to wrap up. The day after they arrived in New York, the building's lobby was transformed into a busy apparel shop where two tailors measured survivors for new navy blue business suits. As was done sixteen years earlier for the *Titanic* crew, shoes, shirts, hats, underwear, neckties and new leather suitcases were issued to each man. Lamport and Holt covered the costs, even though officials at the Institute would have provided everything for free. Each morning, after assembling to receive the day's meal vouchers, most of the crew passed the time by walking around nearby Battery Park, while others took in a movie or two at the theater around the corner. Some wrote letters home. Despite what they'd been through, most of the men weren't overly distraught about what happened. For the most part, the crew viewed the shipwreck as part of the job and they wanted to get back to sea as soon as possible.

Unfortunately for many of them, they first had to get past Charles Tuttle.

As the days wore on, the confrontational Tuttle was having a field day with the *Vestris's* crew. He grilled Adams, MacDonald and Verchere, but saved his heavy ammunition for Johnson. While on the stand, the chief officer related his version of events and blamed the sinking on "exceptionally bad weather," but the U.S. Attorney was having none of it. On more than one occasion, the hapless Johnson struggled with Tuttle bearing down on him. In an exchange over the leaks in the half-doors, Tuttle beat Johnson to a pulp:

> Tuttle: "Are you sure there had never been any place for gaskets?"
> Johnson: "No, I am not sure on that point."
> Tuttle: "As a matter of fact, were not some of those gaskets missing?"
> Johnson: "No."
> Tuttle: "What?"
> Johnson: "No; at least—"
> Tuttle: "You give us an answer to the question I asked you."
> Johnson: "There was nothing missing on the door."
> Tuttle: "I do not care whether nothing was missing. I am talking about gaskets. What have you got on your mind, Mr. Witness? You seem to be hesitating."
> Johnson: "I am not hesitating; I am trying to imagine all these things."
> Tuttle: "What?"
> Johnson: "I am trying to imagine them."
> Tuttle: "You said you had charge and you were the responsible officer for the sealing up of these ports. I do not see why you should have to have much imagination in order to tell us whether any gaskets were missing."
> Johnson: "There was no gasket missing as far as I know."
> Tuttle: "Mr. Officer, you were the first officer on board and in charge of closing these ports, and the lives of everybody on

> the vessel depended upon the closing of these ports properly. Why do you have this difficulty in telling us whether or not there had ever been gaskets on those doors? Is it because you never inspected them?"
>
> Johnson: "Well, we had no trouble with the doors."
>
> Tuttle: "I do not care whether you never had trouble with the doors; you had plenty of trouble with them on this voyage. I am asking you a simple question."

Tuttle proved he could be combative with witnesses, but he also revealed himself to be a neophyte when it came to his knowledge of ships and shipping. He struggled with basic terminology and the investigation stalled at critical times because of his unfamiliarity with the layout of the *Vestris*—details not lost on the British press. However, even more glaring than what was learned was the information that was left out. Johnson and the others were questioned on topics ranging from the ship's coaling ports to her notorious list, but the subject of overloading was never really addressed. In one fleeting instance, Tuttle asked a Lamport and Holt manager if the *Vestris's* draft was "all right." The man answered "Yes," and Tuttle moved on.

Nevertheless, the British were thoroughly fed up with Charles Tuttle. Liberal Member of Parliament Sir Hamar Greenwood diplomatically called on the Americans to change their ways:

> A British ship is a part of the Empire and the loss of a British ship is a loss to the Empire. All we seek of our American kinsmen is that they treat our witnesses before their proper tribunal as they would be treated in this country.

British newspapers were even more direct. The *Evening Star* called the proceedings a "scandal," complaining Tuttle was "densely ignorant of nautical matters." *The Daily News* fired the heaviest broadside. Under the headline "*The Tyranny of Mr. Tuttle*," the paper minced no words in assailing his tactics in the courtroom:

LAST DANCE OF THE VESTRIS

He shouts at witnesses, accuses them of lying, and when he thinks he has scored points he grins in triumph. The bullying, biased, ignorant and inconceivably stupid procedure suggests inevitably a preconceived resolve to condemn and vilify British seamanship and the conduct of British officers at all costs and in the face of all proof to the contrary.

The *News* saved its best for last:

Mr. Tuttle, this silly and bombastic State Attorney who has not yet discovered the difference between a vessel's port and starboard side, will not succeed, even if he tries, which seems extremely improbable, in the distanglement of facts from falsehoods.

Dickerson Hoover closed the Steamboat Inspection Service investigation on December 1. Carey was faulted for waiting too long to call for help and for his failure to provide "a strong directing hand" throughout the emergency. Hoover also found the officers of the *Vestris* didn't "seem to measure up to the standard that we would expect to be present in a British ship." Perhaps most remarkably, Hoover overlooked his inspectors' blatant malfeasance and exonerated Edward Keane and the others. "There was no evidence at the hearings that the loss of life was due in any degree to failure of the inspectors in the performance of their duty," Hoover wrote. He also found no evidence to support accusations they imbibed liquor while enjoying the hospitality of the *Vestris's* crew.

Instead, Hoover blamed that same crew for the loss of life. He faulted operator error for the breakdown of the rusty and corroded equipment his inspectors certified as being in good condition a week prior to the sinking. "Some reference has been made to the failure of the releasing gear to function," Hoover wrote. "But it is reasonable also to suppose, with the lack of discipline that was apparent at the time, that the crew apparently were entirely unfamiliar with the use of the gear." Hoover also rejected the half doors and coaling ports as possible locations of the fatal leak and determined that a ruptured scupper pipe running along the interior of the ship's hull plates was responsible for the sinking.

After hearing testimony from fifty witnesses over the course of two weeks, Tuttle's inquiry also came to an end. In his closing argument, Captain William H. Coombs of the British Officers' Federation addressed Commissioner O'Neill and expressed confidence the investigation would reveal there was nothing Carey and his men could have done to prevent the loss of life. He begged that the "gallant" *Vestris* officers, "tired and seaworn," not be made the scapegoats of the disaster:

> I ask you to remember that those officers appeared here with clear consciences, and with a desire to help you in the service of humanity. You will, I feel sure, stand convinced that there has been no attempt at mental reservation; they have striven to tell you all they know.

Coombs had obviously been left out of the sessions at the Hotel Holley.

A week before Christmas, O'Neill released his findings to a public that was demanding answers. Surprisingly, Lamport and Holt employees came off better than they did in Hoover's report. "The crew seems to have been competent if led, but they were not properly led," O'Neill wrote. Carey took a beating. The captain was hammered for making a number of deadly mistakes: pumping out the bilge tanks; waiting too long to send the distress signal; failing to give the alarm to go to boat stations; ignoring boat assignments; failing to man the boats properly and loading passengers into the port boats while their starboard counterparts were largely ignored. O'Neill wrote:

> The argument that because of the great list of the vessel, the passengers could not have safely been brought down from the port side is without merit. The list would not have been so great if

so many precious hours had not been wasted in the disastrous attempt to use the port boats.

Perhaps most notably, O'Neill determined the *Vestris* was *not* overloaded. It was a huge victory for Lamport and Holt and their expensive lawyers. The sessions paid off.

The weeks of intense press coverage and public outrage moved humorist Will Rogers to offer his two cents. At the conclusion of the Tuttle inquiry, the legendary wit took to the pages of *The New York Times* to affix blame for the sinking once and for all:

> That *Vestris* investigation certainly turned in a thorough report. They said the ship was wrong, the crew was wrong, the captain was wrong, the inspectors were wrong, England was wrong, America was wrong, the ocean was wrong. The only thing they failed to criticize was the thing that caused it all, that was the weather.

The *Voltaire* arrives in New York Harbor two days after the *Vestris* went down. (*Bain News Service*)

After being interviewed repeatedly by reporters and giving testimony at the inquiries, survivors began the process of getting on with their lives. Former Second Class passenger A.C. Patterson had planned to sail for South America on the *Voltaire*, but ended up on the Munson Liner *Southern Cross* along with Paul Dana, Herman Rueckert, William Burke and Joseph Twomey. At least one of them had no fear of being shipwrecked again. "Just according to the law of averages we have nothing to worry about," Twomey said. "I don't believe anything like the *Vestris* disaster could happen twice in succession."

While the *Southern Cross* was preparing to depart her own Hoboken pier, an enterprising reporter found his way on board and located half of the Pluckiest Pair in his cabin. He asked Paul Dana if he would answer a few questions. "Mr. Dana is not yet aboard," Dana snapped. The reporter respectfully disagreed; explaining that since Dana's picture had been flooding the streets of New York for so many days, there was no way he could expect anonymity. Finally, Dana broke down and admitted he had been interviewed so many times he was simply out of things to say. As the ship steamed out of New York Harbor, Paul Dana was finally on his way to the assignment he would have claimed weeks before had he not been delayed by the *Vestris* sinking. The mild-mannered RCA executive must have been eager to put the nightmare he endured behind him for good, because Dana would never see Clara Ball again.

Dana and the others left the country at about the same time fugitive survivor Ovelton Maxey discovered he would have no choice but to remain stateside for the foreseeable future. Maxey, who had been in the water two hours before being plucked out by lifeboat No. 13, was recovering from exposure in a Manhattan hotel room when a pair of detectives dropped by to haul him off to Bellevue Hospital's prison ward. Maxey was miserable. While he waited to be taken back to Virginia to answer for his crimes, he also had to battle an infection related to a recent vaccination and the high fever that went along with it. As they took him away, the policemen told Maxey how they caught up with him—by following his movements in newspaper coverage of the disaster.

CHAPTER SEVENTEEN

"He Proved Himself a Hero"

Michael O'Loughlin was celebrated on both sides of the Atlantic for staying at his post while the *Vestris* keeled over. On the afternoon of November 18, New York City came out to pay tribute to his memory. Nearly two thousand mourners joined representatives of the British Marconi Company, RCA and surviving *Vestris* crew members for a memorial service at Wall Street's Trinity Episcopal Church. In an editorial, Dublin's *Irish Independent* newspaper lauded O'Loughlin:

> We are proud of the fact that again an Irishman has done his duty, putting all thoughts of his own safety aside. Men of other nations would have done as much. An Irishman, true to the traditions of his race, would do no less.

There was also plenty of glory for the wreck's biggest hero. Alfredo Ramos praised the courage of Quartermaster Lionel Licorish and summed up the feelings of the other *Vestris* passengers whose lives he saved. "That little Negro did what the officers of the *Vestris* failed to

"HE PROVED HIMSELF A HERO"

do," Ramos told a reporter. "The quartermaster was the only member of the crew who exerted himself in our behalf."

Much to his own embarrassment, Licorish had become the toast of New York City. Two weeks after the *Vestris* went down, the wealthy and powerful came out to show their appreciation. A reception at City Hall was held by Mayor Jimmy Walker to award the quartermaster the New York City Medal and Scroll. Licorish was the first to speak. He set a serious tone, touching on the topic of "duty," but he wrapped up his remarks with a line that garnered laughs and thunderous applause. "The Americans treat me so nice that I hope I never get out of sight of them," he joked.

Lionel Licorish poses on the deck of the *American Shipper*. (*Associated Press*)

LAST DANCE OF THE VESTRIS

When Licorish finished speaking, Mayor "Beau James" went to the lectern to praise him:

> When you left that ship and reached out your hands to save someone else's life, it is fair and reasonable to suppose that no one asked you what race you belonged to—no one asked you where you were born and no one was interested in your color. They were mighty glad to have your arms around them and they were mighty glad to accept the assistance you brought them.

His Honor concluded his remarks with a call for tolerance:

> I am rather inclined to believe that if we did a little more, while the ship was sailing safely, if we had the same willingness to accept assistance and the same absence of discrimination, then this would be an even greater country than it is today.

On the first weekend of December, Licorish was the guest of honor at a ball held at Harlem's Rockland Palace. Five thousand turned out to pay homage, including British Consul General Sir Harry Gloster Armstrong. As the evening dragged on, Licorish wanted to go to bed, but he stayed and spent hours shaking hands with the men who couldn't wait to meet him and dodging the ladies who kept trying to kiss him.

Also that weekend, New York Congressman Royal Hurlburt Weller announced his intention to introduce a bill calling for Licorish to be awarded the Congressional Medal of Honor. Weller said of the quartermaster, "He proved himself a hero." Unfortunately, it wasn't to be. Three months later, Weller was dead and the driving force behind the effort to decorate Licorish was gone.

Vaudeville companies cashed in on the disaster by signing surviving crewmen to contracts and sending them out to share their stories with eager audiences. Three stokers were paid $65.00 a week for a tour of a few weeks. Even Licorish took to the stage, doing three shows daily at Manhattan's Hippodrome Theater. The gig was just the tip of the iceberg. A grueling schedule required him to speak five additional times a day at theaters throughout the city. In addition, because his fame extended across the country, Licorish found himself in demand at theaters in Chicago and Boston. The financial details of his contracts weren't disclosed, but it's safe to say Licorish probably made more money on stage than he did at the helm of the *Vestris*.

The sinking had become a cultural phenomenon with the tiny quartermaster at the center. Country music pioneers Frank Luther and Carson Robison were having a breakout year in 1928 and ballads about news events were a big part of their success. Robison wrote the haunting *The Sinking of the Vestris* while Luther provided the vocals:

> *Proudly she sailed from New York City,*
> *Bound for a land o'er the sea;*
> *And on her decks were wives and husbands,*
> *And children with hearts gay and free.*
>
> *They sailed on their way o'er the deep blue ocean,*
> *Never a thought of fear;*
> *For there on the bridge stood Captain Carey,*
> *A sailor for many a year.*
>
> *Then come the storm that hit the Vestris,*
> *Wild waves come rolling high;*
> *And there in her side a hole was pounded,*
> *Then they knew that death was nigh.*
>
> *Slowly they sank as the Captain waited,*
> *Hoping his ship he could save;*
> *And then too late he sent the message,*
> *The Vestris was doomed to her grave.*
>
> *Sad were the cries of men and women,*
> *Mothers with babes held so tight;*
> *Brave men who fought to save their loved ones,*
> *Lifeboats that sunk in the night.*

LAST DANCE OF THE VESTRIS

Great was the toll of lives that was taken,
Husbands and wives torn apart;
And many a home with loved ones missing,
Many a sad, broken heart.

There on the deck stood the gray-haired Captain,
Waiting for death to befall;
And though we know that someone blundered,
We should forgive after all.

We are all adrift on life's mighty ocean,
Where each mistake has a cost;
And we should learn from this sad story,
If we hesitate we are lost.

It wasn't their only *Vestris* record. Luther and Robison followed it up with *The Heroes of the Vestris*. This time the songwriter didn't mention Captain Carey:

This song is a tribute to bravery,
To those who were tried and found true;
When the great ship the Vestris was sinking,
Far out on the ocean blue.

Their names have been written in history,
Where the deeds of the brave never die;
And surely a crown will be waiting,
When they face the great master on high.

O'Loughlin was one of the heroes,
Who went to a cold ocean grave;
But he stayed at his post in disaster,
The lives of the others to save.

"HE PROVED HIMSELF A HERO"

And there was a strong little Negro,
As brave as a hero could be;
He worked with the strength of a demon,
And saved twenty lives from the sea.

Brave mothers clung to their babies,
Brave husbands clung to their wives;
Praying that God spare their loved ones,
Willing to give up their lives.

All through the long night they struggled,
Fought with their hands cold and numb;
Trying to save one another,
Praying that help soon would come.

Great ships were rushed to the rescue,
And there in the cold break of dawn;
They saved what was left of the victims,
But more than a hundred had gone.

Oh let us pause for a moment,
We who are free from all tears;
And pay our respects to the heroes,
Whose brave deeds live on through the years.

In addition to the special attention paid to Licorish, the female survivors were being hailed as heroines—not only for their courage and calm in the face of danger, but also for the sense of style they brought to the shipwreck narrative. When asked about the ladies he rescued, *Wyoming* skipper Overstreet told a reporter, "The vitality of those five women was really rather remarkable." The hairpins, narrow shoes, shrinking blue dresses and shopping trips left a positive impression on a public looking for a silver lining to the sometimes sickening story. Manhattan's *Panorama Magazine* summed it up best in an editorial entitled "The Saner Sex." Dr. A. A. Brill wrote:

> So long as a woman carries a vanity case, [a man] has no fears for her safety. The women on the *Vestris*, tossed by a rotten hulk of a boat, swamped in water two-miles deep, torn from husbands and children, beaten upon by rain and wind, have gone through an experience that will undoubtedly leave indelible scars upon the nervous systems of their men companions. They came out of it with a sanity that asked for lipsticks before food, for manicures before surgery. There seems little reason to fear for a group each one of which, when photographed on board the rescuing steamers, wore her blanket a la Chanel, and her sailor's cap with a kind of cockeyed glory.

The day after Madame Inouye arrived in New York from Virginia, her dead husband was promoted posthumously to Lieutenant Colonel by the Japanese Government. He was also eulogized by a U.S. Army Colonel in a joint Christian and Buddhist ceremony at the Manhattan chapel of the National Casket Company. More than a hundred people were there, including representatives of the Japanese army and navy. Madame Inouye attended in a wheelchair, still suffering the effects of exposure. After the service, Inouye's ashes were sent home to Tokyo.

On the second Tuesday after the wreck, a cortege of hearses pulled up in front of Hoboken's Trinity Episcopal Church for a funeral service honoring seven of the *Vestris's* crew. The event was attended by survivors who were still in town and by hundreds of members of the community. Surviving *Vestris* sailors and *Voltaire* crewmen served as pall-bearers, carrying the Union Flag-draped coffins out of the church before gently lifting them into the hearses for the four mile drive to Hoboken Cemetery. The somber parade was led by police officers and was followed by mourners in two busses. Butcher Harry Hawkins, 50; Trimmer Andrew Seales, 32; Stewards Frank Rigg, 36; Bridgeman Harley, 23 and John Owen, 34; Fifth Engineer John Jones and Bartender Thomas Jones were laid to rest. They were all Englishmen, with the exception of Seales, who was the lone Barbadian. Only Rigg's brother, Thomas Jones's sister, and three relatives of Harley were able to attend. The remaining victims were buried by the gathering of strangers.

The women of the *Wyoming*. From left to right: Mary Ulrich, Marion Batten, Elvira Rua and Dolores Doril. Madame Inouye is in the ship's hospital. (*Wide World*)

A week after Paul Dana left town, the *Voltaire* sailed for South America, carrying the majority of the *Vestris's* Barbadian crewmen and a dozen or so surviving passengers including Herbert Johnston, Dr. Ernst Lehner, Alfredo Ramos and Edward Walcott. The *Voltaire* carried 325 passengers, a total the company touted as being the second largest number ever to be carried by the ship. Lamport and Holt couldn't resist mentioning the fact the line received sixty new reservations and only five cancellations in the weeks following the *Vestris* sinking. The company also went to great lengths to make sure the *Voltaire* was shipshape for the voyage. As she steamed out of New York Harbor, her lifeboats were noticeably brighter with fresh white paint, their ropes coiled on deck and ready for action—if the need for them arose.

With the American inquiries in the books and the dead buried, it was finally time for the rest of the crew to go home. Johnson and Watson slipped out on the *Majestic*, while Second Butcher John Keown and twenty-four other survivors boarded *Celtic* for Liverpool. Keown was fortunate to be alive, having survived fifteen hours in the water before being hauled into a lifeboat and eventually rescued by the *American Shipper*. What happened next would test whether his luck would hold.

As the *Celtic* prepared to make an early morning call at Cobh, Irish Free State, to land mail and passengers, the *Vestris* contingent found themselves in peril once more. The harbor pilot was unable to come aboard due to seventy mile per hour winds, driving rain and heavy seas. In his absence, the captain tried making a run for it past the rocks off Roche's Point. It turned out to be a bad idea. Disaster struck while Keown and nearly everyone else slept. A massive gust of wind pushed the *Celtic* onto the rocks. The ship struck with such violence, terrified passengers were thrown from their bunks. Keown woke to the sound of women screaming and the sensation of the ship shaking violently. Far below, seawater poured into the engine room through huge tears in the *Celtic's* side and bottom.

As alarm bells rang, sailors wasted no time in uncovering the lifeboats, swinging them out and then lining up to man them. The operation went like clockwork. There was no panic as passengers calmly went to their assigned stations. Consistent with White Star's reputation for understatement while preparing to leave a stricken ship, one steward went around politely asking, "Gentlemen, why not get on your life belts?" As it turned out, there would be no need to abandon the *Celtic*. Nervous passengers were relieved to learn the ship was not in danger, so they made their way back to their cabins to shed their life belts before heading to the dining rooms for breakfast.

The *Vestris* men were eventually sent home by boat to Liverpool, where a crewman shared his belief the shipwrecks could be blamed on bad luck. Second Wireless Operator James MacDonald was convinced there was a Jonah among the *Vestris* contingent. "I have a good idea who he is," he told a reporter. "But I don't like to mention his name."[9]

Despite several attempts to free it, the great ship never made it off the rocks. The first-built of White Star's famed "Big Four" was finished. Within a few months, the *Celtic's* hulk would be broken up for scrap.

In the wake of the *Vestris* disaster, the Board of Trade had a silver salver engraved for Captain Cumings, to thank him for his seamanship and courage while rescuing more than a hundred unfortunate passengers and crew. The only problem was, he couldn't accept it—and it would take nearly ten years and an Act of Congress before he could. In addition to his everyday job with the American Merchant Lines, Cumings served in the U.S. Navy Reserve. At the time, federal regulations prohibited officers from receiving gifts from foreign governments. Consequently, Uncle Sam held the tray and more than 200 other awards until the House and Senate voted to change the law in May, 1936. A few months later, a box arrived at Cumings's Yonkers home containing the award—along with a letter requesting that the captain write to confirm he'd received the tray.

---

[9] In nautical superstition, a "Jonah" is someone who brings bad luck to a vessel. It has its origin in the Bible story of Jonah who spent three days in the belly of a whale.

CHAPTER EIGHTEEN

"Only the Strong Had a Chance of Being Saved"

Representatives of the Board of Trade spent the five months immediately following the *Vestris* sinking gathering as much information as possible for their own investigation. Beneath crystal chandeliers and gilt ceiling, Wreck Commissioner Butler Cole Aspinall opened the inquiry in the Great Hall of London's Royal Society of Engineers building on April 15, 1929.

With a look around the room, one could safely assume the members of this court *would* have command of basic nautical terminology. An entire wall was covered by giant reproductions of the *Vestris's* original plans. Microphones and speakers were installed to help everyone hear the testimony more easily. The wreck commissioner himself was a heavyweight in the shipping world. Aspinall played a major role in every shipwreck inquiry of the early 20th century. He had the distinction of representing the Board of Trade at the *Titanic* inquiry, served as counsel for Canadian Pacific Railway at the inquiry into the loss of the *Empress of Ireland* and represented the Cunard Line during

"ONLY THE STRONG HAD A CHANCE OF BEING SAVED"

the *Lusitania* proceeding. With the likes of Aspinall running the show, it was no wonder the British considered Tuttle and Hoover to be amateurs.

In direct contrast to the Americans, the Board of Trade wasted no time getting to the heart of the matter. By the second day, the court was discussing Plimsoll lines and heard evidence the *Vestris* departed New York in an overloaded condition. Even Captain Heasley testified the ship should not have been allowed to go to sea with the extra tonnage from the "preference list" on board. The inquiry was zeroing in.

E.A. Digby, attorney for Captain Carey and both the surviving and deceased officers asked Heasley if anything sinister happened at the Hotel Holley, "Were you not suggesting a draft which had no existence in fact?"

"I did nothing of the kind," Heasley answered emphatically.

The investigation moved on. A few days after Heasley left the stand, it was Johnson's turn. For the third time in a row, the chief officer made an unsympathetic witness, and he would fare no better in London than he did in New York. However, his experience would be markedly different. This time, Johnson held nothing back:

> We were having continual discussions on board the *American Shipper* regarding the draft. We did not want the American people to get hold of this overloading business and were trying to conceal it. That was our intention from the beginning. We wanted to get home, not to remain all the time in the American courts.

Johnson even brought up Cumings's admonishment to be loyal, saying, "Well, we tried to be, that was all."

"And you are still anxious to be loyal?" Aspinall interrupted.

"Well, I cannot be!"

Predictably, the chief officer's testimony caused a firestorm across the Pond. The New York *Telegram* attacked him for being "the most embarrassed, the most nervous and the most evasive of all the procession of witnesses here." Even so, the paper expressed hope Johnson's confession was an indicator of a positive result:

> The dam of secrecy and deceit broken, more of the concealed truth about the death and untold suffering which engulfed the passengers who sailed so happily from this port on the *Vestris* six months ago may be forthcoming.

An enraged U.S. Attorney Tuttle said he would look into the possibility of bringing Johnson back to the United States to face charges. It also gave him a golden opportunity to counterattack the British press that had treated him so harshly:

> During the course of the American inquiry there was some criticism in the English newspapers based on the alleged fact that in examining Mr. Johnson and some of the other officers of the vessel I had pressed the witnesses too hard. I cannot but feel that the recent disclosures made by Mr. Johnson are a full answer to such unwarranted criticism.

However, since Tuttle never asked him about the draft, Johnson couldn't have perjured himself. The erstwhile chief officer stayed in England.

On the fourteenth day, Stephen Southam, onetime first officer of the *Vestris's* sister ship *Vauban*, lowered the boom on his former employers when he revealed how turning a blind eye to overloading was practically Lamport and Holt policy:

> It has been the practice to load these ships with apparent disregard of safety and stability. In my opinion this ship [the *Vauban*] has left New York seriously overloaded, and it has been part of my duty to falsify the log abstracts so that it was recorded that the ship sailed properly loaded when, in fact, she did not.

Southam also told of being reprimanded by his own chief officer when he recorded the "wrong" draft. "I was told to cut it out and use liquid ink eraser and write in another draft on top," he said.

"ONLY THE STRONG HAD A CHANCE OF BEING SAVED"

In the end, the three surviving officers' testimonies turned out to be the most interesting installments in the otherwise highly-technical proceeding. As expected, the surviving wireless operators and engineers gave evidence. Dozens of stewards and sailors also took the stand. Second Steward Alfred Duncan, who tried so hard to make passengers comfortable that fateful morning, offered sobering insight as to why so few women and children survived. "My only suggestion is that the women were not able to help themselves when in the water," he said. "The position was such that only the strong had a chance of being saved."

After hearing from sixty-six witnesses and reading nearly two dozen affidavits into the official record, the inquiry came to a close. The forty day proceeding set a record—eclipsing the length of the *Titanic* inquiry by three days. Butler Aspinall read the Court's findings on the last day of July, but despite the massive amount of testimony, the wreck commissioner expressed disappointment that all the facts about the *Vestris's* fatal voyage might never be learned. "Speaking generally, the evidence is unsatisfactory, contradictory, inconsistent and piecemeal," Aspinall said. "Much of it is unreliable, some of it is untruthful."

Aspinall went on to give several reasons the *Vestris* was lost, chief among them overloading, the top heavy condition of the ship and the leaks in the ash ejector and half doors. Uncovered hatches and bad weather were also blamed. The theory of the broken scupper pipe, named as the culprit by the Hoover inquiry, was discounted. The Court also condemned The Order that Should Not Stand as being "highly undesirable," and recommended it be done away with.

The wreck commissioner addressed Carey's actions after expressing regret the captain was not present to defend himself. "While the Court were not forgetful that the captain was a shipmaster of experience and good repute, it thinks his conduct in relation to the boats is open to some criticism," Aspinall said. Carey was blamed for waiting too long to send out the SOS, in addition to his "unwise" decision to load the portside boats, but in the end the captain was found not guilty of having committed wrongful acts. The Court also vindicated the *Vestris's* firemen. Aspinall found "no lack of order among the crew or any particular section of the crew." Johnson was cleared for the part he played in the sinking, although it was determined he was "remiss" in the way he handled the flooding in the cross alleyway. Chief Engineer Adams and the Lamport and Holt Line were likewise found blameless for their actions.

Instead, Captain Heasley, David Cook and Lamport and Holt Marine Superintendent Harry Wheeler were each found guilty of wrongful acts for allowing the *Vestris* to go to sea overloaded. Cook was ordered to pay the Board of Trade £500 to cover costs related to the investigation, and that was that. The three were the only people to be held criminally responsible for the sinking of the *Vestris*.

In the months following the disaster, the spotlight had gradually dimmed on the shipwreck *The New York Times* once called "The grimmest epic of the seas since the *Lusitania* was sunk." Consequently, reaction to the Board of Trade's findings in the United States was tepid. *Time* Magazine yawned, "*Big Blame, Small Penalty*," while the *Washington Post* lamented the disaster's lack of staying power:

> Nine months have elapsed since the *Vestris* sank off the Virginia Capes carrying 112 souls to their deaths. In the interval, public interest in the disaster has largely disappeared. The Board of Trade report is looked upon impersonally today, whereas in the days immediately following the tragedy it would have been examined critically and made the basis for a demand that its recommendation be given the force of law.

When Frank Johnson admitted he and the others lied by omission at the American inquiries, it was only a matter of time until Lamport and Holt ships were made unwelcome in American ports. Upon learning of the testimony, Congressman Fiorello LaGuardia became incensed. He wanted the line banned "in the face of the startling and repulsive testimony brought out at the board of inquiry in London." The flamboyant Republican from East Harlem fired off a letter to the

"ONLY THE STRONG HAD A CHANCE OF BEING SAVED"

Secretary of Commerce to demand Lamport and Holt vessels be prohibited from sailing into or from U.S. harbors. In his conclusion, LaGuardia became the only government official to level the accusation Sorensen and others once threw around freely, "The sending out of this ship with human lives in order to collect freight and passenger fees was nothing short of cold-blooded murder."

A Lamport and Holt spokesman dismissed the letter, telling reporters LaGuardia was "talking wildly." He went on to mention reservations were unaffected by what had transpired in London. What he failed to say was that bookings had fallen off since the *Vestris* sinking overall, and that Lamport and Holt was struggling with severe financial problems. The company was well on its way to losing $350,000 in 1929.

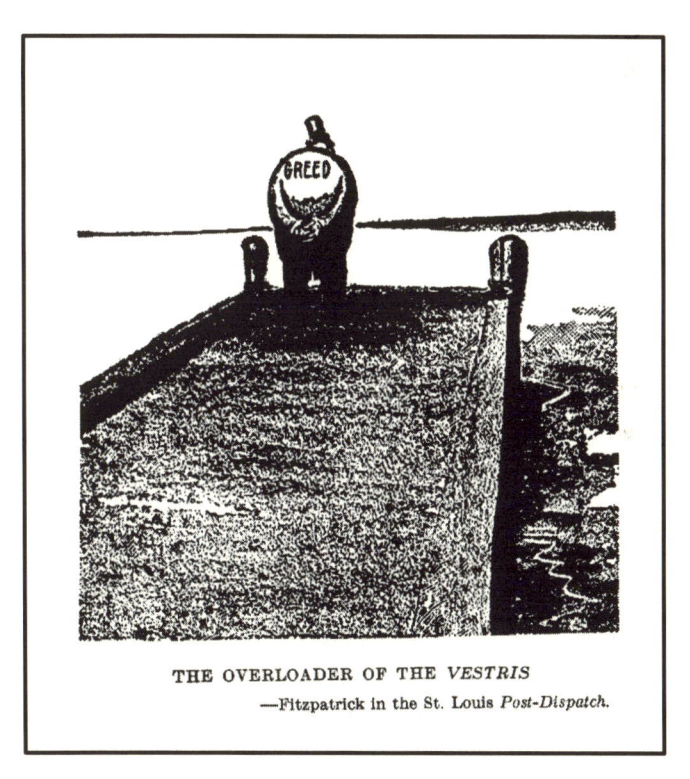

THE OVERLOADER OF THE *VESTRIS*
—Fitzpatrick in the St. Louis *Post-Dispatch*.

This cartoon was also featured in the May 25, 1929 edition of *The Literary Digest*. (Author's collection.)

LAST DANCE OF THE VESTRIS

As it turned out, increased competition and the economic crisis accomplished what the congressman could not. The year after the *Vestris* went down, the supremacy of Lamport and Holt's *V-Class* liners was challenged in a palpable way by Furness Withy's Prince Line, which added four new vessels, and from the popular Munson Liners already on the South America route. On a late summer day in 1929, the *Voltaire's* crew arrived in New York Harbor to learn Lamport and Holt had decided to pull the plug on further voyages. A press release explained why:

> The continued depression in the trade between New York, Argentina, Brazil and Uruguay is such that the operation of vessels possessed of large passenger-carrying capacity is not warranted and the board of directors of Lamport & Holt, Ltd., after due consideration, has decided to withdraw these two fine vessels until such time as the passenger trade revives.

Seven freighters remained on the route, but the *Voltaire* and *Vandyck* were recalled to England and mothballed. As Lamport and Holt's parent company came apart financially, the precious mail contracts that had been a source of pride and revenue for the company for more than six decades were sold off. Left unable to pay its bills, Lamport and Holt was placed into the hands of a receiver.

The familiar ships with the light blue and white funnels would never again carry passengers past Manhattan skyscrapers, nor would cheerful orchestras play as the liners steamed down the North River. Travelers had no choice but to use a different shipping line to take them to exotic South America because in the end, LaGuardia's wish came true. The last dance of the *Vestris* was the tragic opening act in a drama that saw the curtain come down on Lamport and Holt's South America passenger service for good.

CHAPTER NINETEEN

"These Men All Died In Storm and Terror"

More than a hundred years after the *Titanic* went down, Lower Manhattan remains dotted with monuments to that ship and those who perished on her. One of them sat atop the Seamen's Church Institute for decades—a 60 foot tall, working lighthouse that was eventually moved to its current home at the South Street Seaport Museum. At the time of its construction, the museum's magazine stressed the need for such a memorial, because "in a busy, careless city the average person so soon forgets."

Unfortunately, there aren't any memorials to the *Vestris* or to her victims; no bronze statues or elaborate stained glass windows like the one the Astor family commissioned for their lost loved one. In the *Vestris's* case, the editorial writer was correct—the busy public forgot in short order. Perhaps it was the minor loss of life in comparison to the *Titanic* that caused the disaster to fade, or maybe it was just bad timing. The sinking may have been eclipsed by the stock market crash and depression less than a year later or the outbreak of the Second World

War in 1939. Whatever the reason, the *Vestris* and her passengers were left behind as the 20th century marched on.

However, a member of the ship's crew *is* memorialized in Lower Manhattan, and the plaque on which he is remembered forever binds the *Vestris* to her larger cousin from Belfast. Soon after the disaster, Michael O'Loughlin's name became the twenty-fourth to be added to the Wireless Officers Monument in Battery Park, below Jack Phillips of *Titanic* fame. The inscription reads:

MICHAEL J. O'LOUGHLIN
S.S. VESTRIS
NOVEMBER 12, 1928
OFF VIRGINIA COAST

The white granite cenotaph was constructed with money raised in the wake of the *Titanic* tragedy. Hundreds attended its dedication in 1915, including novelist Willa Cather. She wrote about it in an article for *Sunday Magazine* entitled "Wireless Boys Who Went Down with Their Ships:"

> The monument is one of the most attractive and most friendly commemorative works in New York, and, unlike most of our monuments, it is beautifully placed—and humanly placed. It is a single pilaster with a loop of sea-shells and sea-wood across the front, and the names of the wireless men. This cheerful monument has a peculiar attraction for the children who live in the neighborhood of the Battery. They sleep on the stone benches in the afternoon and play on them all the morning, and spell out the names of the wireless men and the ships on which they went down. These men all died in storm and terror; but their names are brought together here and abide in a pleasant place, with cheerful companionship.

Recently, the monument was placed in storage while city construction crews attempt to breathe new life into the run-down Battery. When the marker is rededicated sometime in 2014, the *Vestris* will make her symbolic return to Manhattan. The ship's name and that of the man who gave up his life to save her passengers and crew will be immortalized in New York City once more.

APPENDIX A

"The Gold Ship"

George Holt and William James Lamport bought their first ship in 1845. Twenty years later the men founded the Liverpool, Brazil and River Plate Steam Navigation Company, Limited. Despite its official name, the company remained known popularly as the Lamport and Holt Line. Their ever-increasing number of ships pioneered trade with ports on South America's east coast and the company ultimately won lucrative mail contracts from both the British and Brazilian governments.

By the turn of the 20th century, the company George Holt and William Lamport founded led the shipping industry once more when it inaugurated the New York-to-Brazil and River Plate passenger service. The route proved so popular that by 1910, the company was preparing to add three larger ships to their fleet in an effort to keep up with demand.

Executives picked Workman-Clark and Company of Belfast to build them. At the time, the city was home to two major shipyards, Workman-Clark, known to locals as the "Wee Yard," and Harland and

Wolff, builders of the White Star Line's famous Olympic-class steamers. Quite literally, the two shipyards were close competitors. They were located next door to one another on Queen's Island. Their geographic proximity meant Yard No. 303, eventually the *Vestris,* was constructed in the shadow of *Olympic* and *Titanic.* While the more famous of her larger cousins went on to a catastrophic maiden voyage in April of 1912, the *Vestris* successfully completed her first trip in September of that year, traveling from Liverpool to New York, via the River Plate.

The steamship *Vestris* was a 10,494 ton passenger and cargo liner of the shelter deck design. She was 495 feet long and had a beam of sixty feet, six inches. Workman-Clark built the vessel to be just as modern and luxurious as the monsters steaming out of their neighbor's yard. Lamport and Holt bragged about the *Vestris* and her sisters in a 1913 brochure:

> No expense was spared in equipping these steamers with every convenience for the comfort and amusement of their passengers and for every safeguard for their protection. Special cabins have brass beds and private baths. The handsome entrance hall, the dome and windows of which are of tinted glass, has a mahogany staircase. The saloon, which runs the width of the ship, is provided with cozy tables accommodating four, five or six persons.

Shipbuilder magazine, which famously profiled the *Titanic* in 1911, also devoted space that year to describing the *Vauban*, the *Vestris's* nearly-identical sister:

> The First Class passenger accommodation is situated amidships, the staterooms being large and well-appointed, with a number being situated on the tandem principle. The public rooms include the dining saloon with small tables, music room with lounge adjoining, and smoking room with an open-air Veranda Cafe at the after end. There is also a nursery adjoining the dining

saloon. The accommodation for Second Class passengers comprises large staterooms with handsomely furnished dining, music and smoking rooms. A gymnasium, barber's shop and electrically-driven machinery are provided.

The ship's two quadruple-expansion reciprocating steam engines burned more than a hundred tons of coal a day. At full speed, her twin screws propelled her along at a clip of 14 ½ knots. For the convenience of passengers and crew, the *Vestris* was equipped with an automated laundry room and electric fans and lighting throughout.

Much more important to Lamport and Holt's bottom line than the passenger trade was the transport of frozen meat. The company's vessels had been carrying the cargo since the 1880's and the *V-Class* liners were not exempt from the duty. The *Shipbuilder* continued:

> The cargo space is divided into five holds, practically free of obstruction. Some of the cargo compartments are insulated and fitted up for the carriage of chilled meat, fruit and produce, with an efficient installation of coolers and fans.

Unfortunately, the *Vestris* had a serious design flaw. She was severely top heavy, or "tender." The problem was so pronounced a thirty-five mile per hour wind on her quarter automatically gave the ship a five-degree list, and if she tilted eleven degrees, her scuppers dipped into the sea. A maritime expert would later say that under the right—or wrong conditions, the ship could become a deathtrap.

During the Great War, the *Vestris* was pressed into service on behalf of the Allied cause. Her hull was painted battleship gray and her funnel black. The ship contributed to the war effort by transporting mostly munitions and supplies across the Atlantic. On one frightening occasion a German torpedo meant for the *Vestris* missed its target, but for the most part her four years of service were uneventful until her final wartime voyage. Joy and pain were felt after a crossing from New York to Havre, France with eight hundred war nurses aboard. It was at the beginning of the Spanish Flu outbreak, which would ultimately kill

"THE GOLD SHIP"

off otherwise healthy young adults by the tens of millions. The *Vestris* wasn't immune.

The deadly virus mixed with her human freight of twentysomethings and created a deadly combination. The flu incapacitated nearly everyone on board and eight nurses died. Crewmen buried the unfortunates at sea; the rest were landed safely where, as it turns out, they weren't even needed. As the ship departed for France after a stop at Dartmouth, a critical message was received via semaphore: "To Master *Vestris*, hostilities will cease at 11 a.m. G.M.T. today, November 11, 1918. You will proceed on your voyage burning navigation lights, avoiding all traffic as much as possible, and cease zigzagging. Report immediately any suspicious vessel to nearest radio station." When word was passed, cheering and hat throwing broke out.

A line-crossing ceremony aboard the *Vestris* c. 1914. The swimming tank was wood-framed with canvas sides and bottom. When filled, it added five degrees to the ship's list. (*Mike Poirier*)

LAST DANCE OF THE VESTRIS

After the Armistice, the *Vestris* found herself part of an unfamiliar fleet. The Cunard Line needed help dealing with an increased volume of westbound passenger traffic, so the company chartered the *Vestris* and her sisters from Lamport and Holt. The agreement required the ships to ferry passengers under the Cunard flag from Liverpool to New York before reverting back to Lamport and Holt to take passengers and cargo to South America, and then return to England packed with frozen meat.

It was on one of the first southbound voyages when, in September of 1919, the *Vestris* made international news. Two days out of New York, a fire was discovered smoldering in one of the ship's coal bunkers and despite their best efforts, the crew couldn't put it out. The cruiser *HMS Yarmouth* escorted the burning *Vestris* to the Caribbean island of St. Lucia, helped extinguish the fire, and then pumped the excess water out of the charred liner. No one was hurt, but the experience was a nightmare for the 450 passengers who had to be landed and lodged in army barracks until the ship was pumped out and repaired. There was a bright side. The *Vestris's* crew went ashore with supplies and served passengers four sumptuous meals a day. After ten days the ship was in good enough shape to resume her voyage. The arrangement with Cunard turned out to be so successful, the sisters helped the company break postwar records for the number of passengers carried. After six circuits, the *Vestris* returned permanently to serving Lamport and Holt and the South America route she knew so well.

During her heyday, New York reporters nicknamed the *Vestris* "The Gold Ship," for being the vessel of choice of South American governments looking to transfer millions of dollars in gold bullion to banks in New York City. Incredibly, the massive shipments' dates of departure and arrival were reported in the papers along with the amount of gold on board. Despite such open invitations to piracy, the *Vestris* completed her seagoing armored car assignments without incident.

The Lamport and Holt Line had been added to the portfolio of Lord Kylsant's Royal Mail Steam Packet Company around the time of the *Vestris's* maiden voyage. By 1928, and with the recent acquisition of the White Star Line, the RMSPC was easily the biggest shipping company in the world, controlling many of the best known lines of the era. The *Vestris* was registered in Liverpool but based in New York, where Lamport and Holt's day-to-day operations were subcontracted to the American firm of Sanderson and Son, Ltd. While her owners in England made regulations and hired and assigned ship's officers, the U.S. managers were responsible for passenger reservations and cargo bookings. Sanderson and Son was also charged with keeping the *Vestris* in good working order, a critical duty that, as events would prove, was not always carried out.

APPENDIX B

Passengers and Crew

Names of persons saved are
italicized in bold.

FIRST CLASS

William P. Adams
Norman K. Batten
Marion Batten
Leah Brownfield
Wyatt A. Brownfield
William B. Burke
Margaret A. Daugherty
Paul Dana (Ayrault)
William Wills Davies
Earl Devore
Anne Devore
Iracema Dos Santos Cabral
Alfred C.E. Fletcher
Antoinette Fletcher
Carlos Franke
Mrs. Carlos Franke
Ingeborg Franke
Helmuth Franke
August Groman
Charles M. Henrotin
Herman Hipp
Yoshio Inouye
Teruko Inouye
Ernest Alonzo Jackson
Jannette B. Jackson
Cary Jackson
Agnes E. Johnson
Edward F. Johnson
Herbert C. W. Johnston
Arthur M. Jones
Campbell Kellman
Sidney S. Koppe
Ernst Lehner
Thomas E. Mack
Edward John Marvin
Ovelton L. Maxey
Mabel M. Mills
Isaac Nahen
Ernesto G. Permuy
Carl L. Pfaff
Charlotte Puppe
Fred W. Puppe
Lisolette Puppe
Carlos Quiros
Lloyd R. Ricketts
Herman Rueckert
Wallace M. Sinclair
Cline F. Slaughter
Wilma Slaughter
Walter Spitz
Orrin S. Stevens
Gladys Stevens

PASSENGERS AND CREW

Charles I. Wade Stone
Joseph Forbes Twomey
Clyde C. Persful
Edward Miles Walcott
Edward J. Walsh
Ralph Whitehead
Joseph Benjamin Wilson
Mary Denan Wilson
Francis Wilson
Paul Wilson

SECOND CLASS

Joseph E. Belgrave
Keith W. Burt
Samuel Cox
Helen Cubbin
William M. Fields
C.M. Harris
Mr. Goodman
Sarah J. Goodman
David H. Huish
Iris Johnson
Germaine Julien
Daphne Julien
Arthur C. Patterson
J.E. Pollard
Alfredo Ramos
Clytie K. Raphael
Fredrik Sorensen
J.F. Thompson
Mary Ulrich
Otto Ulrich

THIRD CLASS

Gaetano Abbadini
Jeremiah Alleyne
Mrs. Jeremiah Alleyne
Edgeworth Alleyne
Huntley Alleyne
Lillian Alleyne
Mary Alleyne
Solomon B. Baunoff
S. Bowen
Beulah Bowen
Walter Cadogan
Dalrymple Leslie
Pietro DiConza
Juan Doril
Dolores Barriero Doril
Jorge doValle
William Eversley
Mrs. William Eversley
Harry Fay
James Headley
Mrs. James Headley
Mildred Headley
Marion Headley
Audrey Headley
Nora B. Kanan
Michael Khoriaty
Louis Leuthauser
Mrs. Louis Leuthauser
Vincenzo Murri
Francisco Placente
Mrs. Francisco Placente
L.E. Ramos

LAST DANCE OF THE VESTRIS

Marion Reid
Theophilus Rowe
Jose Gonzales Rua
Elvira Rua
Jorge Rua
John Santana
Carl Schmidt
Clarence Smith
Mrs. Clarence Smith
Henry Schultz

Darnley Thorne
Eleanor Parker
Lloyd Keiser
Ramon Garcia Pelal

DEPORTEES

Sarah Leacock
James Cleary

OFFICERS

William John Carey, Captain
Frank William Johnson,
   Chief Officer
John Oswald Bolger
   First Officer
Leslie Watson,
   Second Officer
Herbert George Welland,
   Third Officer

SEAMEN

Joseph Alexis
Archibald Bannister
Reginald Bannister
George Blades
Robert Chase
Elton Clarke
Alexander Crick
William Dyer

Reynolds Federingham
Percy Gibson
Frederick Gill
Granville Gill
Charles Harris
Conrad Helford
St. Claire Hunter
Myrick John
Sinclair Jordan
Lionel Licorish
Joseph McDonald
Gladstone Messiah
Arthur Prescott
Leonard Reach
Warwick Roberts
Grafton Sargeant
Joseph Smith
Percy Waldron

MARCONI COMPANY

Michael Joseph O'Loughlin,
    Chief Operator
*James T.F. MacDonald,
    Second Operator*
*Charles Verchere,
    Third Operator*

HOSPITAL

Dr. William Sears, Surgeon
*Hugh Lewis Jones,
    Attendant*

BAND

Andrew Bartozzi
Edwin Conrad
Ray Royal
Conrad Werner

ENGINEERS

*James Avard Adams,
    Chief Engineer*
John Blue, Second Engineer
*Harry Forsyth,
    Third Engineer*
*George Prestwich, Fourth
    Engineer*
John Jones, Fifth Engineer
*Reginald Dickson, Sixth
    Engineer*

*Miller Watson,
    Seventh Engineer*
*Jose Garcia,
    Eighth Engineer*
Sidney Holme,
    Chief Refrigerating
    Engineer
*Ernest Smith,
    Second Refrigerating
    Engineer*
Thomas Fulton, Electrician
Egbert Boice, Donkeyman
Sidney Hassell, Donkeyman
Alexander McClaggan,
    Donkeyman

FIREMEN

Gerald Burton
Joseph Boxill
George Carter
Donald Dettin
St. Claire Estwick
Gilbert Ford
Thomas Ford
George Frank
Evans Hampden
Joseph Hinds
Donald Holder
William Monroe
John Morris
James Oliviere
Samuel Parfitt
Samuel Ramsey

Clarence Scott
Theophilus Sealey
Joseph Shaw
James Straughan
Gerald Straughan
Reginald Weekes

COAL TRIMMERS

James Atkins
James Chase
Charles Cladier
Joseph Garner
Cuthbert Craig
Ben Cutting
Fritz Gittens
Cyril Greenridge
Samuel Headley
Charles Harris
Clarence Hunt
James Niles
Andrew Scales
Hendry Vanderpool
McDonald Wells

GREASERS

Aubrey Batsen
Leonard Bennett
Joseph Clarke
John Hedrington
Alexander Hurdle
William Pearman
Robert Rose

Harrington Williams

STEWARDS

Richard Davies,
    Chief Steward
Alfred Duncan,
    Second Steward
Clara Ball, Stewardess
Thomas Boyd
John Bramwell
Suppert Brown
J. Byrne
George Coles
Alfred Cohen
Alfred Dineley
Ernest Dobbison
Thomas Edwards
Thomas Evans
William Foran
Bridgeman Harley
Randolph Harris,
    Engine Steward
George Hogg
John Hornby
Andrew Hough
Percy Hudson,
    Deck Steward
Edward Howard
Robert Jarvis
Murde Kenzie
John Kipling
Albert Knill
Erwin Leschaloupe,

PASSENGERS AND CREW

Bath Steward
James Littlemore
Enrique McCullock
Laurinda Moore,
  Stewardess
Wallace Ernest Mercer
William Millard,
  Lounge Steward
Gilbert Owen
John Owen,
  Bedroom Steward
Claude Pay
Donald Phillips
Oscar Preston,
  Captain's Servant
James Ray
Frank Rigg,
  Chief Bedroom Steward
Thomas Robinson,
  Bedroom Steward
John Ross
Samuel Sadowski
Isaac Scott
Harold Vowles
Charles Walter
Alfred Watson
Arthur Williams

GALLEY

George Amsdell, Storekeeper
David Anderson, Baker
Christenson Bird, Baker
Felix Blanc, Pantryman
John Henry Burn,
  Entrée Cook
Ernest Carpenter,
  Second Cook
Walter Chapman, Baker
Neville Connor, Cook
Edward Darcy, Chef
Jean Gladianes, Pantryman
Alfred Hanson, Pantryman
Harry Hawkins,
  Chief Butcher
Hubert Hunt, Cook
Ralph Jones, Cook
John Keown,
  Second Butcher
Coleridge Licorish, Cook
William Little, Cook
Antonio Maradigue,
  Pantryman
Aaron Medlfca, Storekeeper
Thomas Moffatt,
  Chief Baker
Horace Moore, Cook
Marvin Neal, Cook
Griffith Pritchard, Cook
Joseph Spitzer, Fruitman

OTHER CREW

Aloysius Banfinch,
  Night Watchman
John Braithwaite, Dayman
Stanley Brown, Linen Keeper
Brownhill

Harry Clevenger, Barber
Thomas Connor, Waiter
Henry Daley, Bellboy
M. Dixon
Stoney Ford, Laundry Boy
John Grainger, Waiter
Thomas Griffin, Waiter
Charles Harris, Lamps
Clifford Jones, Servant
Edgar Jones, Servant
Sidney Jones, Foreman
Thomas Jones, Barman
David Lockett,
    Carpenter's Mate
James McCulloch,
    Laundryman
Margaret McCulloch,
    Laundress
William McDonough,
    Baggage master
William Perman, Grater
G. Pride,
    Engineering
Albert Pugh, Chief Purser
Victor Segre, Printer
John Winstonley,
    Night Watchman
Gustav R. Wohld, Carpenter

APPENDIX C

Twin-Screw Steamship "VESTRIS"
Length, 512 Feet. Displacement Tonnage, 17,000
PLAN OF FIRST CLASS ACCOMMODATION

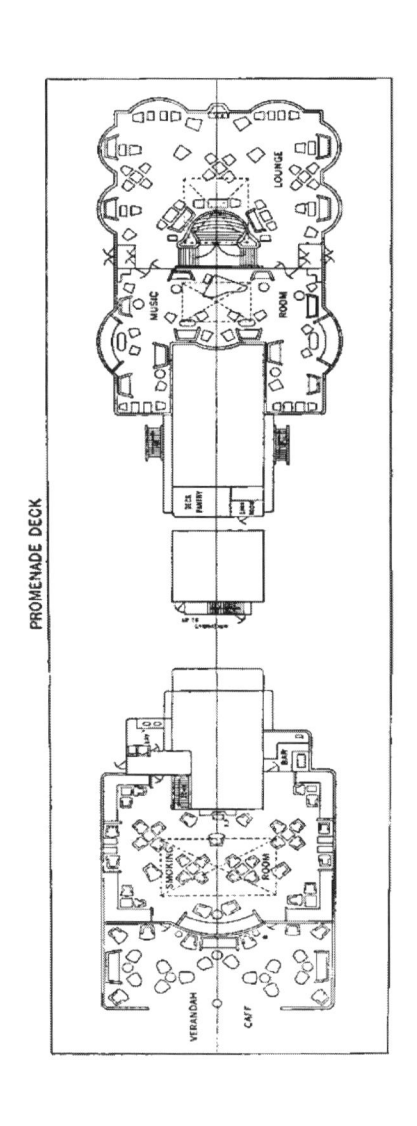

LAST DANCE OF THE VESTRIS

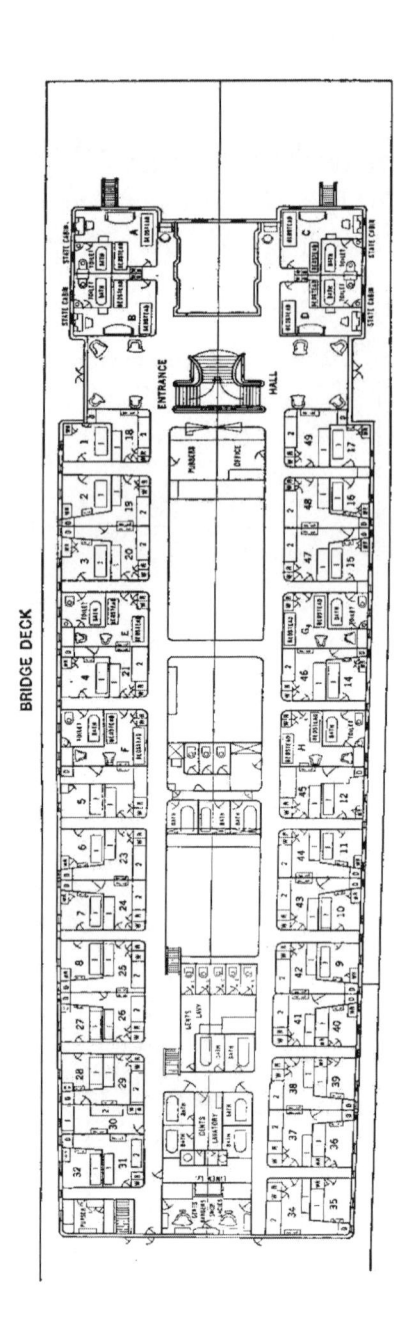

DECK PLANS

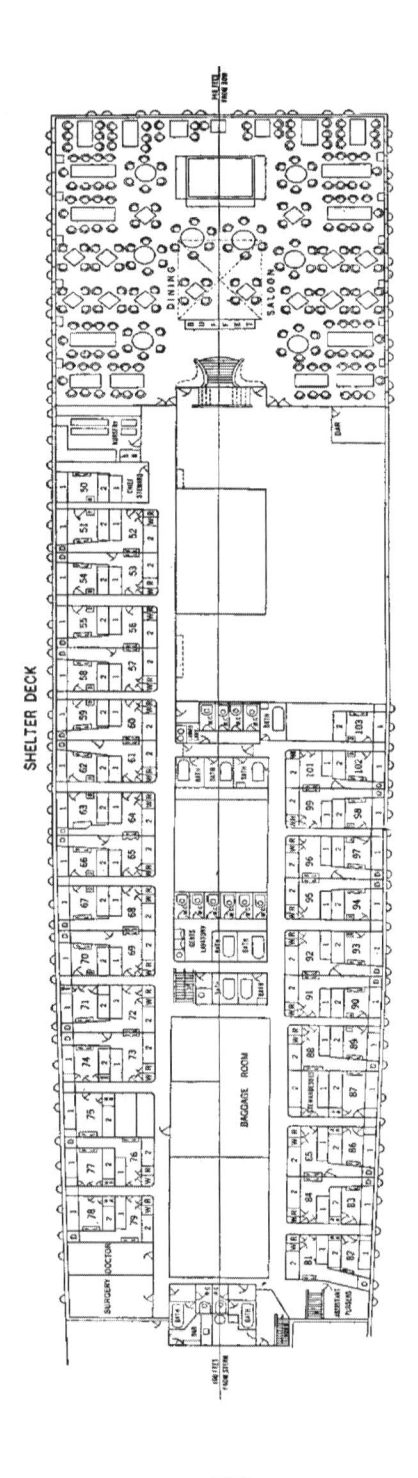

185

BIBLIOGRAPHY

BOOKS

Baarslag, Karl, *SOS to the Rescue*. New York: Oxford University Press, 1935.

Barnaby, K.C., *Some Ship Disasters*. New York: A.S. Barnes and Company, 1970.

Cozzens, James Gould, *S.S. San Pedro*. New York: Harcourt, Brace and Company, 1931.

Forgotten Shipbuilders of Belfast. Belfast: Friar's Bush Press, 2004.

Hadfield, R.L., *Sea-Toll of Our Time*. London: H.F. & G. Witherby, 1930.

Heaton, Paul, *Lamport & Holt Line*. Abergavenny, Monmouthshire, Great Britain: P.M. Heaton Publishing, 2004.

Hoehling, A.A., *Great Ship Disasters*. New York: Cowles Book Company, Inc., 1971.

BIBLIOGRAPHY

Lord, Walter, *A Night to Remember*. New York: Holt, Rinehart and Winston 1955.

Report of the Board of Trade Inquiry into the Loss of the Vestris. Liverpool: Journal of Commerce, August 1929.

Riesenberg, Jr., Felix, *Yankee Skippers to the Rescue*. New York: Dodd, Mead & Company, 1940.

Warren, Mark, *Distinguished Liners from the Shipbuilder, Vol. II*. New York: Blue Riband Publications, 1997.

MAGAZINES

Barry, Peter. "Loss of the Vestris." *Sea Breezes* April 1986: 282-288.

"Catastrophe: Vestris." *Time* November 26, 1928

Collins, Charles. "Photografy Classic Tells the Story of an Ocean Tragedy." *Grafic Magazine* 22 February 1953: 4.

"Datafile Lamport and Holt." *Ships Monthly* January/February 2011: 37-48.

Hucker, Robert. "The Vestris Disaster." *Sea Classics* July 1979: 72-82.

Kneen, Beryl and Orville. "The Flying Cameraman." *Popular Mechanics* September 1928: 378-383.

Markey, Morris. "The Sinking of the Vestris." *Panorama* November 24, 1928: 6-7, 22.

Meister, Brian J. "RMS Vestris, Ship of sorrow, ship of shame." *Voyage Quarterly* October 1990: 70-74.

"Truth of the Vestris Tragedy at Last." *The Literary Digest* May 25, 1929: 10.

Rowbotham, Mark. "Forgotten Fleets: Lamport and Holt." *Shipping* June 2009: 52-61.

Whitelock, Otto. "S.O.S. Vestris." *Argosy* February 1960: 58-59, 74-78.

Wolfe, George D. "The Last Hours of the Vestris." *Ships and Sailing* September 1951: 44-50.

NEWSPAPERS

Atlantic Daily Bulletin, Baltimore Sun, Baltimore News, Boston Globe, The Bound Brook Chronicle, Brooklyn Daily Eagle, Chicago Tribune, Christian Science Monitor, Danville Bee, Hartford Currant, Indiana Evening Gazette, Ipswich *Evening Star, The Illustrated London News, The Lincoln State Journal, Los Angeles Times, Manchester Guardian,* British *Daily News, New York Daily News, New York Herald Tribune, New York Post, Omaha Bee-News, The Pittsburgh Press, Rockford Republic, Scarsdale Inquirer, St. Louis Post-Dispatch, The New York Times, Salt Lake Tribune.*

DOCUMENTS

U.S. District Court, Southern District of New York, Petition of The Liverpool, Brazil & River Plate Steam Navigation Co., Ltd. and Lamport & Holt, Ltd. for limitation of liability, as owners of the S. S. *Vestris*. Opinion of Goddard, D. J.

Shipping casualties. Loss of the steamship "Vestris." Report of a formal investigation into the circumstances attending the loss of the British steamship "Vestris" of Liverpool, in the Atlantic Ocean in or near latitude 37 35 north and longitude 71 08 west, on November 12th, 1928, whereby loss of life ensued. British Board of Trade, London.

BIBLIOGRAPHY

Steamship "Vestris." Report of United States Commissioner Francis A. O'Neill on the investigation into the causes and circumstances of the sinking of the steamship "Vestris."

Steamship "Vestris." Report and recommendations of Dickerson N. Hoover, Supervising Inspector General, made to the Secretary of Commerce of the investigation held in New York City, November 20, 21, 22, 23, 27, and December 1, 1928, of the accident to the steamer "Vestris."

ARCHIVAL RESOURCES

Bronx, New York, SUNY Maritime College Stephen B. Luce Library, Archives and Special Collections, Alumni, Personal Papers of Schuyler F. Cumings.

Columbia, South Carolina, University of South Carolina Libraries, Moving Image Research Collections, Fox Movietone News Collection, News Stories C7456, 1-428, 1-429, 1-448, 1-449.

WEBSITES

Jackson, R. (2006, January 20). *Jackson Vestris Papers Index*. Retrieved March 2, 2010, from http://patriot.net/~eastlnd/rj/vestris/jpvi.htm.

Darrah, F. (2005, January 4). *The Vestris Disaster*. Retrieved March 2, 2010, from http://bluestarline.org/lamports/vestris.html

ACKNOWLEDGMENTS

I'm especially grateful to my wife, Alisha, for the constant support she provided me as this project unfolded over the course of more than three years. I also cannot begin to express enough appreciation to Jack Gallon and Josh Reed for their assistance in producing this volume.

Thanks also to veteran researchers Jim Kalafus and Mike Poirier, who were a limitless source of information, guidance and moral support. I also wish to thank Ardis Parshall and Ramon Jackson for graciously sharing the accounts and information they compiled about *Vestris* passengers. The book also benefitted greatly from the assistance of author Roy "Lean and Hungry" Fenton, and Shafeek Fazal and Elizabeth Berilla at the Stephen B. Luce Library at the Maritime College of the State University of New York. Thank you for caring about my work.

I would like to express my appreciation to Terence Curtis for his assistance with some critical research, and to Patrick Becker of ABC News and Sheena Brown, Deputy Director of Art and Antiquities at the New York City Parks & Recreation Department. Thank you for being my eyes and ears on the ground in the *Vestris's* home port.

ACKNOWLEDGMENTS

And lastly, I will be forever grateful to Cunard Line Commodore Ronald Warwick, who I first met on board the QE2 in 2008. Thank you for your gracious foreword as well as the technical expertise only you could provide.

ABOUT THE AUTHOR

Clint Olivier is an award-winning journalist whose work has appeared in print and has aired on television and radio. His assignments have taken him everywhere from New Orleans in the immediate aftermath of Hurricane Katrina, to the site of the Mountain Meadows Massacre in Utah to California's Mojave Desert for the landing of Space Shuttle Discovery.

Olivier has crossed the Atlantic Ocean on board the *QE2*, visited the location of the *Titanic* disaster and has sailed on vintage ocean liners constructed by both John Brown & Company of Clydebank, Scotland and Harland and Wolff. He writes from Fresno, California.

Printed in Great Britain
by Amazon.co.uk, Ltd.,
Marston Gate.